GRAMMAR WORKOUT

28 Lessons, Exercises, and Activities to Jump-Start Your Writing

STUDENT ACTIVITY TEXT

Catherine DePino, Ed.D

J. WESTON
WALCH
PUBLISHER
Portland, Maine

Dedication

To my parents, Mary Grace and EJ Spinelli,
for showing me the beauty of the English language.

"There is no frigate like a book."—*Emily Dickinson*

Acknowledgements

Heartfelt thanks to Lisa French, an expert and a creative editor-in-chief, and to Holly Moirs, a talented and conscientious editor, who is always there with a smile and a helping hand.

1   2   3   4   5   6   7   8   9   10

ISBN 0-8251-4250-4

Contents

To the Student

Grammar Workout will help you learn all the grammar you need to know. With this knowledge, you'll speak and write with ease. Short explanations and fun exercises will help jump-start your language skills. You'll soon be a pro with both oral and written English.

What You'll Need to Get Started

Before you start your grammar workout, you'll need some basic equipment. You'll need a portfolio for storing your assignments and projects. Be creative with your portfolio. You can use a manila envelope or a large folder with pockets. You might use a scrapbook or a three-ring binder. You could also use a large gift bag. Make your portfolio special by decorating it with markers and glitter. Add drawings, photographs, or cartoons that you like.

You'll record class notes in a slim notebook. Choose one that fits into your portfolio. Buy a stack of lined paper for your writing assignments. You'll also need a highlighter and colored markers. You'll use these in class and for your homework assignments.

You can also use your portfolio for storing other things. Make room for parent-teacher and student-teacher forms. These forms will make it easy for you and your parent or guardian to keep in touch with your teacher about your work.

Your Learning Style

As you use this book, think about the ways you learn best. Is memorizing an easy way for you to learn? If not, there are other methods you can try. Suppose you have a long list of terms or words to study. First, think about *why* you're learning the list. *See* how the words in the list are used in the examples. *Listen* to all examples discussed in class. *Use* the words in your own examples. By *understanding* and *using* the words in the list, you might learn them faster than if you had memorized the list. You might also remember them longer.

Grammar Workout helps you learn quickly and painlessly in many ways. You will learn with the entire class and in groups. You will work on your own and with a partner. Sometimes you and your partner will e-mail each other for help with writing. A large part of this program is talking about good grammar. This book will help you feel at ease using grammar in writing and speaking.

Grading Your Work

After some homework assignments, you'll find a rubric. The rubric gives you a set of standards for grading the assignment. Use the rubric as a guide to score a piece of writing. Look at the standards in the rubric. Then look at the writing. What is your overall impression? Would you give the writing a *1, 2,* or *3* based on the points in the rubric? *Before you write,* look at the rubric. It will help you know what you need to do to write a great essay or story. Use the rubric to check your work *after you write.* It will give you ideas for revising what you have written.

You will also use the rubrics with your partner or group. You will score and edit each other's papers. The rubrics will help you learn what makes good writing. They will also help you learn how good writing differs from fair or poor writing. You will even create your own rubrics for some assignments. Your teacher will also use the rubrics to grade your revised papers.

Rubrics help you improve as a writer. They tell you what the standards are for each assignment. They show you exactly what you need to do to reach top form. You can then work hard to meet those standards.

Summary

To sum it up, *Grammar Workout* helps you work your grammar muscles. First, it walks you through the different parts of speech. Then it picks up the pace by showing you types of sentences. Lastly, it helps you break through the finish line with sentences that are blooper-free. You won't have to wonder if you've used the correct punctuation. You'll know if you've written a run-on sentence. Like a coach, *Grammar Workout* will push you to the limits so that you reach peak form.

The most important thing you need to succeed in this course is *you.* Bring your special talents to these assignments. Be creative. Push yourself until you reach your goals. Become the best speaker and writer you can be. Enjoy your workout!

Spring into Action with Verbs

Lesson 1: Action Verbs

- **An action verb shows physical or mental action.**

 Think About It: Action Verbs

Every sentence needs a verb to make it complete. There are two main types of verbs: action verbs and linking verbs. **Action verbs** show action you create with your body or your mind. We also call this physical or mental action.

EXAMPLES
Action you create with your body: I *jumped* up in the air to make the basket.
Action you create with your mind: I *know* the answer to your question.

Writing Connection: Using strong action verbs gives your writing power and energy. Using ordinary verbs makes your writing lifeless and boring. Picture the action, and then think of the perfect verb to describe it.

EXAMPLES
Ordinary Verb: The frisky pony **jumped** over the fence. **Strong Action Verb:** The frisky pony **leaped** over the fence.
Ordinary Verb: The peacock **walked** around the zoo. **Strong Action Verb:** The peacock **strutted** around the zoo.

Picture It

Read the story below. Highlight all of the action words in the story. (These action words are all listed in the Word Bank.) Remember, action verbs can show action you create with your body or your mind.

A Test to Remember

Word Bank

start	answered	shouted	pointed
studied	gave	shook	show
growled	jumped	run	sleep
worked	do	handed	
said	wanted	passed	

Yesterday Ms. Crabtree gave us an impossible math test. The night before the test, I couldn't sleep. The day of the test, my stomach growled and my hands shook. I wanted to run from my desk. The girl in front of me passed me the test paper.

Ms. Crabtree pointed to the clock. "Start now."

I had studied hard. Now it was time to show what I could do. Before long, I had answered all the questions but one. The next day the teacher handed me my paper. "You have worked hard. Your grade is a 90," she said. I jumped in the air and shouted. I felt proud and tall.

Practice

Choose an action verb from the Word Bank to complete the story below. Score 10 points for each correct answer. **Score** 90

Gorilla Sundae

Word Bank				
pay	ate	tasted	order	feed
take	threw	drove	shared	share

1. After school Tanya and Jim _____drove_____ to the Super Scoop Ice Cream Parlor.

2. They _____shared_____ a Super Fudge Banana Split.

3. Tanya only _____tasted_____ a bit of the whipped cream and cherries because she wasn't very hungry.

4. Jim _____ate_____ all of the ice cream and hot fudge.

5. Tanya _____threw_____ the banana into a brown bag.

6. "I'll _____feed_____ it to my pet gorilla," she said.

7. "I'll _____take share_____ the banana home and eat it later," Jim said.

8. "Then I'll _____order_____ my gorilla his own Super Fudge Banana Split," Tanya said.

9. "Forget that, Tanya. I will _____share_____ the banana with your gorilla," Jim said.

10. "I refuse to _____pay_____ for a Super Fudge Banana Split for your pet gorilla.

Great Job!

More Practice

Choose the strong action verb that fits best in each sentence. Circle the letter in front of the action verb you choose to fill in the blank. Score 10 points for each correct answer. **Score** _____

1. José and Linda _raced_ home from school. They couldn't wait to go to the amusement park.
   (a) walked
   (b) raced
   (c) strolled

2. Mom met them at the door. "Let's go before it rains," she _urged_.
   (a) urged   *urged*
   (b) said   *(~~says~~ conveys*
   (c) whispered   *excitement)*

3. When they reached the park, Linda _chose_ the Thunderbolt for their first ride.
   (a) liked
   (b) chose
   (c) parked

4. The roller coaster dipped and _swerved_ around the sharp corners.
   (a) slipped
   (b) moved
   (c) swerved

5. "Let's ride the Ferris wheel next," José said. When they got to the top, their seat _rocked_ back and forth.
   (a) rocked
   (b) rolled
   (c) jumped

6. Mom liked the bumper cars best. When she crashed into José's car, he quickly _turned_ his wheel.
   (a) touched
   (b) moved
   (c) turned

7. Next, José and Linda rode the merry-go-round. The horses' heads _bobbed_ up and down.
   (a) hopped
   (b) bobbed
   (c) jumped

8. Mom laughed when a pile of fake snakes _hissed_ at them in the fun house.
   (a) hissed
   (b) laughed
   (c) looked

9. "Let's go on the pirate ship for our last ride," José said. The pirate ship _swayed_ from side to side. So did Linda, José, and Mom.
   (a) growled
   (b) flew
   (c) swayed

10. As the family left the park, a bolt of lightning _flashed_ across the sky, and it started to rain. "We made it just in time," Mom said as they raced to the car.
    (a) ran
    (b) flashed
    (c) slid

 **Homework**

Spelling

Something I Enjoy Doing

Strong action verbs make your writing sparkle. On lined paper or on a computer, write a five-sentence paragraph about something you enjoy doing in your spare time. Use at least four strong action verbs in your story and underline them. Give your story a beginning (one sentence), a middle (three or four sentences), and an end (one sentence). Dream up an interesting title for your story based on the topic. Write a brief outline in the space below before you begin to write. This outline will include your topic sentence and at least three supporting details. You can also add ideas for your ending in your outline.

I Love baseball. It is some thing
I do in my free time. I'm on a team.
Last year I piched a no hiter. I hit
2 dobles, 3 2 singls and strukout
two
14 baters. Baseball is my farret sport.

Scoring Rubric

1. **Top form (You're a champ!)**	2. **Fair (Keep trying!)**	3. **Needs improvement (Don't give up! You can do it!)**
Composes interesting title	Composes fairly interesting title	Composes an uninteresting title
Uses at least four strong action verbs	Uses at least three strong action verbs	Uses fewer than three strong action verbs
Writes excellent topic sentence	Writes good topic sentence	Writes fair-to-poor topic sentence
Supports topic sentence with at least three details	Supports topic sentence with at least three details	Supports topic sentence with fewer than three details
Writes paragraph that has a beginning, middle, and end	Writes paragraph that has a beginning, middle, and end	Writes paragraph that does not have a distinct beginning, middle, and end
Makes no spelling errors	Makes no more than two spelling errors	Makes more than two spelling errors

Great Job—
Try some more descriptive verbs for on, is and do.
Don't forget your punctuation.
Write your spelling words on the left (corrected)

Love you!
mom

Lesson 2: Linking Verbs

- **Linking verbs link the subject of the sentence to another word in the sentence.**

Think About It: Linking Verbs

Hop, run, throw, holler, think, and *believe* are all action verbs. You can picture people creating these actions with their bodies or their minds.

There's another type of verb we use all the time. It's called a **linking verb.** Linking verbs don't express action you can see. Instead, they link the subject of the sentence (what the sentence is about) to another word in the sentence.

EXAMPLES

1. The Doberman seemed angry when I took away his bone. (In this sentence, the word *Doberman* is linked with the word *angry*.)

2. The cat sounded upset when the mouse jumped on her back. (In this sentence, the word *cat* is linked with the word *upset*.)

COMMONLY USED LINKING VERBS

am	was	grow	seem
be	were	look	smell
is	become	remain	sound
are	feel	appear	taste

Writing Connection: It's best to use strong action verbs in your sentences. But there are times when you'll want to use linking verbs.

EXAMPLES: WHEN TO USE LINKING VERBS

1. **When you don't know who is doing the action:**
   A chain letter was sent to my friend.

2. **When you don't want to tell who did the action:**
   The missing papers were returned to my teacher's desk.

Think About It: Linking Verb or Action Verb?

Sometimes you need to do some serious thinking to tell if a verb is linking or action. Look at these two examples using the verb *appeared*:

1. My teacher *appeared* angry when I started to snore in class.

2. When the ghost *appeared*, Hamlet shook and shouted.

You can see that the word *appeared* has a different meaning in both sentences. In the first sentence, you can't see any action going on. Instead, the sentence shows a *state* the teacher is in. In the second sentence, you know there is action because you can picture the ghost appearing to Hamlet.

One way to help you decide if a verb is linking or action is to test the verb by substituting *is* or *was* for the verb. If you can use *is* or *was* in place of the verb, it's a linking verb. Try it with the first sentence, and you'll see that it fits: My teacher *was* angry when I started to snore in class. Try substituting *is* or *was* in the second sentence, too. What do you think?

Picture It

Read the story below. Highlight all of the linking verbs in the story. (These words are all listed in the Word Bank. One word is used twice.)

Mom's Apple Pie

Word Bank					
be	are	smells	is	feel	am

"I am so tired today," Kia said.

"Don't you feel well?" her mother asked. "You are not your usual happy self."

Kia looked around the kitchen. "What smells good?"

"It is an apple pie for you," her mother said.

Kia smiled. "I feel much better now. Today will be a special day."

Practice

Find the linking verbs. In each example below, circle the letter of the sentence (a or b) that has the linking verb. Score 10 points for each correct answer. **Score** _____

1. (a) *Sound* the trumpets! Ring the bells!
   (b) That movie *sounds* exciting.

2. (a) The cafeteria food *tastes* delicious.
   (b) Did you ever *taste* octopus soup?

3. (a) *Look* at that blimp in the sky!
   (b) That elephant *looks* very hungry.

4. (a) The cookies *smell* wonderful.
   (b) I can *smell* the apple pie baking.

5. (a) I *felt* exhausted after swimming 20 laps.
   (b) Dad *felt* my head to see if it was feverish.

6. (a) Chang's crocodile *grew* so long that he couldn't fit in the tub.
   (b) Mother *grew* tired of reminding me to start my homework.

7. (a) My pet spider *looks* hungry.
   (b) "*Look* at that messy room," said Gram.

8. (a) "Your homework *appears* satisfactory," said Ms. Curmudgeon.
   (b) The alien *appeared* from out of nowhere.

9. (a) The students *grew* restless when the speaker kept talking.
   (b) Pinocchio's nose *grew* five inches when he lied.

10. (a) *Look* at that sunset!
    (b) That root beer float *looks* delicious.

Homework

A Funny Thing Happened

Write a five or six sentence journal entry about something funny that happened to you or someone else. Use at least five strong action verbs and two linking verbs. Highlight the action verbs and circle the linking verbs. Write a brief outline here before you write.

_____

_____

_____

_____

_____

_____

_____

_____

_____

_____

_____

_____

_____

Warm-up: Action Verb or Linking Verb?

- **Action verbs show action you create with your body or your mind.**
- **Linking verbs link the subject to another word in a sentence.**
- **How a verb is used in a sentence will help you decide if it's an action verb or a linking verb.**
- **Substitute *is* or *was* for the verb to help you decide if it's an action or a linking verb.**
- **Action verbs move your writing forward and make it more lively.**

Relay Race

Decide if the verbs in *italics* are action verbs or linking verbs. Write *A* for action verb and *L* for linking verb in the space after each sentence. Score 10 points for each correct answer. **Score** _____

1. The sour milk *smelled* disgusting. _____

2. The teacher *grew* impatient when Tyrone wouldn't pay attention. _____

3. After Tamara *tasted* the liver, she gave the rest of it to the dog under the table. _____

4. When the actress *appeared* on stage, everyone clapped. _____

5. The alligator *tasted* so tender that Dion believed he was eating chicken. _____

6. When Marisol *smelled* broccoli cooking, she raced out of the house for a burger and fries. _____

7. Tommy *felt* embarrassed when he forgot to do his homework. _____

8. The cactus *grew* so tall that I had to move out of my room. _____

9. "Do you *remember* those chocolates I bought you?" my friend asked. _____

10. Those pink and yellow seashells *look* beautiful. _____

Lesson 3: Helping Verbs

- **Helping verbs work with main verbs to give different meanings to your writing.**

Think About It: Helping Verbs

Helping verbs like *can, has, should, will,* and *is* work with other verbs to add different meanings to your writing. For one thing, **helping verbs** help you state the time something happens. If you want to talk about something happening in the past or the future, you can use a helping verb to make that clear.

EXAMPLES

1. Miguel *will* jump every hurdle and win. (The helping verb *will* tells us that Miguel will win in the future.)

2. Miguel *has* jumped every hurdle and won. (The helping verb *has* tells you that Miguel has done this before.)

LIST OF HELPING VERBS

Here is a list of commonly used helping verbs. You'll probably remember some of them from your list of linking verbs.

am	were	shall	may	has
is	been	will	might	had
are	do	would	must	
was	did	should	have	

📷 *Picture It*

Read the story below. Highlight all of the helping verbs in the story. (These words are all listed in the Word Bank. Some words may be used more than once.)

Basketball Cake

Word Bank			
been	has	can	have
was	must	were	had

My friend Ryan has been baking cakes for as long as I can remember. He can bake a cake in any shape you want. One day he baked a cake in the shape of a basketball. My sister Jamie was racing through the house while the cake was cooling. She must have thought the cake was a real basketball. While Ryan and I were talking, she threw the cake up in the air. Splat! Bits of cake and icing landed on the floor, the ceiling, and the wall that Dad had just painted.

"What were you thinking?" Ryan asked Jamie.

But she was licking the icing off her fingers. "That must be the best basketball I have ever tasted," she said.

📓 *Practice*

Choose a helping verb from the Word Bank to complete each sentence below. Score 10 points for each correct answer. **Score _____**

Word Bank									
have	will	been	am	must	can	might	would	have	do

"If you _____ like to leave school on time, you _____ straighten out your messy desk," Mr. Quibble said. "I _____ never seen such a mess!"

"I have _____ working hard at school all day. I _____ not feel like tackling this job now. _____ it wait until tomorrow?" Joel asked.

"I _____ tired of waiting. You _____ want to know that yesterday I saw a mouse crawl out of your desk," Mr. Quibble said. "I _____ not want the principal to find out."

"Then I guess I _____ do it now, but only if you help me. I need protection from that mouse," said Joel.

 *Homework*

My Most Exciting Sport

Write a five or six sentence paragraph about your favorite sport. Use at least five strong action verbs and at least two helping verbs. Underline the helping verbs. Highlight the strong action verbs. Write a title and a brief outline of your paragraph here before you begin writing.

_____

_____

_____

_____

_____

_____

_____

Scoring Rubric

1. **Top form (You're a champ!)**	2. **Fair (Keep trying!)**	3. **Needs improvement (Don't give up! You can do it!)**
Composes interesting title	Composes fairly interesting title	Composes uninteresting title
Uses at least five strong action verbs	Uses at least four strong action verbs	Uses fewer than four strong action verbs
Uses two helping verbs	Uses two helping verbs	Uses fewer than two helping verbs
Writes excellent topic sentence	Writes good topic sentence	Writes fair-to-poor topic sentence
Supports topic sentence with at least three details	Supports topic sentence with at least three details	Supports topic sentence with fewer than three details
Writes paragraph that has a beginning, middle, and end	Writes paragraph that has a beginning, middle, and end	Writes paragraph that does not have a distinct beginning, middle, and end
Composes original ending	Composes ordinary ending	Composes boring ending
Makes no spelling errors	Makes no more than two spelling errors	Makes more than two spelling errors

Lesson 4: Verb Tense

- **Tense tells when something happens.**

Think About It: Verb Tense

Verb tense tells when something happens. You are going to learn about three tenses: present, past, and future tense. **Present tense** is happening now. **Past tense** happened before. **Future tense** will happen later. Regular verbs form the past tense by adding *ed* to the main verb (for instance, the past tense of *talk* is *talked*). Form the future tense by adding *will* in front of the verb (the future tense of *talk* is *will talk*).

EXAMPLES

Verb: play
Present Tense:
Andre *plays* kickball every day.
Past Tense:
Andre *played* kickball yesterday.
Future Tense:
Andre *will play* kickball next week.

Verb: dance
Present Tense:
Kelly *dances* in school shows.
Past Tense:
Kelly *danced* in the school show last month.
Future Tense:
Kelly *will dance* in next year's school show.

Picture It

Read the story below. Think about the tense of the verbs in *italics*. Underline the present tense verbs once. Circle the past tense verbs. Put a star above the future tense verbs.

Worm Burger

Shawn *walked* to The Burger Factory for lunch. He *ordered* a triple cheese bacon burger. It *sizzled* on the plate.

"Yum," he said as he *tasted* the burger.

"Yuck!" he *screamed* as he chewed it.

"What *happened*?" asked the waitress. "What is wrong with the burger?"

Jason *showed* her two long and slimy objects. "I *think* I ate worms."

The waitress *started* to laugh. "Those are not worms. They are fried onions. We *serve* them on all our burgers. But I *will cook* you another burger. Would you like one?"

Jason smiled. "Do not bother. I *will pick* the onions out myself."

Practice

Write the tense of each verb in *italics* in the space after each sentence. Score 10 points for each correct answer. **Score** _____

1. Minh and Tim *strolled* to the park. _____

2. "I *want* to go on the swings," said Minh. _____

3. Tim *pushed* Minh higher and higher. _____

4. "Now *will* you *push* me?" he asked. _____

5. Minh pushed him so high that his stomach *churned*. _____

6. "*Push* higher!" Tim shouted. _____

7. "*Will* you *walk* with me to the refreshment stand?" Minh asked after they went on the swings. _____

8. They *sipped* lemonade and ate popcorn. _____

9. "I *will call* my sister to pick us up," Tim said. _____

10. "Do you *want* to come back next week?" Minh asked. _____

 *Homework*

Write a humorous sentence using a present tense verb. Then rewrite the sentence in the past tense and in the future tense, using the same verb. Highlight the verb in each sentence. Remember that a regular verb ends in *d* or *ed*. Here's an example using the verb *nibble:*

Present: The hungry mouse *nibbles* Lauren's toes.
Past: The hungry mouse *nibbled* Lauren's toes.
Future: The hungry mouse *will nibble* Lauren's toes.

Sentence 1:

Present: _____

_____

Past: _____

_____

Future: _____

_____

Sentence 2:

Present: _____

_____

Past: _____

_____

Future: _____

_____

Sentence 3:

Present: _____

_____

Past: _____

_____

Future: _____

_____

Lesson 5: Irregular Verbs

- **Irregular verbs form their past tense differently from regular verbs.**

Think About It: Irregular Verbs

Verbs that form their past tense by adding *d* or *ed* are called **regular verbs.** Some verbs form their past tense by changing into completely different words. These are called **irregular verbs.** Look over the list of irregular verbs. You probably know a lot of them already. But you've also probably heard people incorrectly say *brang* instead of *brought,* or *seen* instead of *saw.* That's because they never bothered to learn irregular verbs.

SOME FREQUENTLY MISUSED IRREGULAR VERBS

Present	Past	Present	Past	Present	Past	Present	Past
am, be	was, were	draw	drew	know	knew	sit	sat
begin	began	drink	drank	make	made	speak	spoke
bite	bit	eat	ate	ride	rode	steal	stole
break	broke	fly	flew	ring	rang	swim	swam
bring	brought	freeze	froze	run	ran	swing	swung
burst	burst	give	gave	say	said	take	took
catch	caught	go	went	see	saw	think	thought
choose	chose	grow	grew	shake	shook	throw	threw
come	came	hear	heard	show	showed	wear	wore
do	did	hide	hid	sing	sang	write	wrote

EXAMPLES: REGULAR VS. IRREGULAR VERBS

Regular Verb:
The baby *giggled* when I tickled his feet. (Past tense of *giggle* formed by adding *ed.*)

Irregular Verb:
Phong's friends *threw* him in the pool. (Past tense of *throw* formed by changing it into another word, *threw.*)

Picture It

Read the story below. Highlight all of the irregular verbs in the story. (These words are all listed in the Word Bank. Some are in present tense; some are in past tense. Some words may be used more than once.)

The Big Catch

Word Bank			
see	throw	was	said
took	am	think	give
do	shook	take	did
catch	were	is	have
eat	went	caught	
began	be	heard	

One day Drew and his friend Carlos went out to sea in a fishing boat. Their goal was to catch a flounder to eat for dinner. As the day wore on, they began to think that all the fish were asleep.

All of a sudden, Carlos shouted, "Give me some help, Drew. I think I caught one."

"No, Carlos. You did not catch a flounder. It is much too heavy to be a flounder. Plus, I see a lot of arms on your fishing pole. Throw it back in the water."

"It took me all day to catch it, and I am not letting it go," Carlos said.

Drew shook his head. "I have heard of filet of flounder, but I do not think I could eat filet of octopus."

Carlos reeled it in. "I'll take it to school. This octopus is a lot more interesting than that inch worm we dissected last week in science class."

Practice

Choose an irregular verb from the Word Bank that fits each sentence. Score 10 points for each correct answer. **Score** _____

Word Bank				
do	give	swim	saw	know
threw	made	take	sing	be

1. Aisha _____ a penny in the fountain at the mall.

2. She closed her eyes and _____ a wish.

3. When she opened her eyes, she _____ a leprechaun standing in front of her.

4. "_____ this magic ring. It will bring you what you wish for."

5. Aisha said, "I want to be able to _____ like my friend Monica."

6. The leprechaun laughed. "Silly girl. She probably wants to be able to _____ like you do."

7. "You may _____ right," Aisha said.

8. "I will _____ you the magic ring back."

9. "I _____ now that I have everything I need."

10. The leprechaun smiled. "You _____ not need me or the magic ring because you have yourself. And that is all you will ever need."

 ## *Homework*

A List of Instructions

Write a six- to seven-step list of instructions for an activity (how to swim, ride a bike, etc.). Use the same irregular verb in at least two different tenses. Try writing a humorous sentence for your final step. Use the past tense. For example: *I rode my bike up a six-foot mountain using this method.* Underline the irregular verb and label the tenses you use in your instructions. Number your instructions. Keep them short and simple, and write them in an order than makes good sense. Give your instructions a title. Make notes for your instructions in this space.

_____

_____

_____

_____

_____

_____

_____

_____

_____

_____

_____

_____

_____

_____

Warm-up: Verbs

- **Action verbs show action you create with your body or your mind.**
- **Linking verbs link one word to another word in a sentence.**
- **Helping verbs work with main verbs to add a different meaning to the sentence.**
- **Verb tense tells about the time something happens: past, present, or future.**
- **Regular verbs add *ed* to form the past tense.**
- **Irregular verbs do not form the past tense by adding *d* or *ed*. They change to a different word to form the past tense.**

Relay Race

Follow the directions before each set of five sentences. Each section has a separate set of instructions. Score four points for each correct answer. **Score** _____

Part 1: Highlight the action verbs in each sentence. You'll find the number of action verbs at the end of each sentence.

1. Whenever company comes, Funny Face, our cat, jumps up on the table and meows. (3)
2. One day she ran over to the kitchen counter and sniffed at the roast beef. (2)
3. My friend and I chatted and forgot about Funny Face. (2)
4. "Help!" my friend shouted in the middle of a sentence. She pointed at Funny Face. (3)
5. When I turned around, I saw that my cat had eaten half of the roast beef. (3)

Part 2: Circle the five linking verbs in the story. In one sentence, a linking verb is used as a helping verb. Write *none* at the end of this sentence.

6. Trong looked bored.
7. "What is the problem, Trong?" Ms. Spitfire asked.
8. "When is this grammar going to get exciting?"
9. "Are you saying that you do not like grammar?" asked Ms. Spitfire, who was getting ready to spit fire.
10. "Oh, no, Ms. Spitfire. You know that grammar was always my favorite subject, and you have always been my favorite teacher."

Part 3: Highlight the helping verb or verbs in each sentence. Remember that sometimes other words come between helping verbs and the main verb. Highlight the helping verbs. Find the number of helping verbs listed at the end of each sentence.

11. Are you going to the winter dance? (1)

12. I did not see many of my friends there last year. (1)

13. They have been talking about going to this dance. (2)

14. They can hardly wait to see the "mystery guest" with the "corn cob pipe and the button nose." (1)

15. I think the mystery guest may be Mr. Popovitch, the science teacher, wearing his Frosty the Snowman suit. (1)

Part 4: Tell whether each *italicized* verb is present, past, or future tense. Fill in the space at the end of the line with the correct tense.

16. My grandparents *told* me that they walked five miles to school in ten feet of snow. _____

17. I *take* the bus, which picks me up at my door. _____

18. I *will walk* to school tomorrow because it will be sunny. _____

19. When it snows, I probably *will* not *have* school. _____

20. Life *was* so much harder in the olden days. _____

Part 5: Write the past tense of each *italicized* irregular verb in the space after each sentence.

21. Ari *drinks* three bottles of water after the relay race. _____

22. Alison *swims* twenty laps at the swim meet. _____

23. Malik *brings* his brother candy worms for a surprise during half time. _____

24. Kwan *goes* in the locker room to get changed. _____

25. Lena *eats* six hot dogs at the baseball game. _____

Get Ready to Roll with Nouns and Pronouns

Lesson 1: Common Nouns and Proper Nouns

- **Common nouns name any person, place, thing, or idea. Proper nouns name specific persons, places, things, or ideas.**

Think About It: Common Nouns and Proper Nouns

All nouns name persons, places, things, or ideas. **Common nouns** name any person, place, thing, or idea. **Proper nouns** name a specific person, place, thing, or idea. Always capitalize proper nouns.

Nouns can tell about one person, place, or thing (book, computer, game, belief). We call these **singular nouns**. Nouns can tell about more than one person, place, thing, or idea (books, computers, games, beliefs). We call these **plural nouns.**

EXAMPLES OF COMMON NOUNS:

Person: student, teacher, friend, singer
Place: arcade, mall, school, seashore
Thing: television, tiger, backpack, car
Idea: honesty, kindness, peace, friendship

EXAMPLES OF PROPER NOUNS:

Person: Toni Morrison, Kwan, Martin Luther King, Jr., George Washington
Place: California, England, Lincoln High School, Mississippi River
Thing: New York Yankees, Statue of Liberty, World Series
Idea: The Great Society, Buddhism, Protestantism

Writing Connection: Specific nouns make your writing more interesting and fun to read. You could use the noun *dog*, but *Dalmatian* would help your reader clearly picture what you are trying to describe.

Picture It

Read the story below. All of the nouns are in *italics*. Put a *C* above the common nouns and a *P* above the proper nouns. Circle the plural nouns.

Beware of the Cat

Rosa and *Josh* couldn't wait to explore the haunted *house* on *Walnut Street*. They walked up the *steps* and knocked on the *door*. A large black *cat* glared out the *window* at them. A *man* dressed in a butler's *suit* answered the *door*.

"May I help you? My name is *Dexter*," he said.

"Yes," said *Rosa*. "We have heard about your famous *mansion*. Can you give us a *tour*?"

"Certainly," *Dexter* said. "But I must warn you. *Percival*, the *cat*, told me that he does not like *guests*. He sometimes traps *people* in the *basement*. As a matter of fact, the last *guests* who explored the *mansion* disappeared without a *trace*. *Percival* was the last one to see them. But he won't talk about it. I can't imagine why. We have been *friends* for years."

"Maybe we'll come back another *day*," *Josh* said. "I don't like *cats*, especially ones that talk."

Practice

Choose a common or proper noun from the Word Bank to fill in the blanks. Cross off the nouns as you use them in sentences. Number 6 and number 10 need two answers at 5 points each. Score 10 points for all other answers. **Score** _____

Word Bank				
lunch	food	cheese	grapes	container
school	sandwich	chance	soup	box
Rayna	Willie			

1. _____ opened his lunch bag.

2. "Oh, no. A cheese _____ again," he said.

3. "Would you like to trade?" _____ asked. "What do you have?" Willie asked.

4. Rayna smiled. "I'm not telling. You just have to take a _____."

5. "Let me see what other _____ I have," Willie said.

6. He reached inside the box. "I see _____ and chocolate cookies. I like them, but I am sick of _____."

7. Willie looked at Rayna's lunch _____. "Let's trade," he said.

8. He looked inside. "What is in this _____?" he asked.

9. "Split pea _____ and tofu sandwiches," Rayna said.

10. "My favorite _____!" Willie said. "I think I'll save it for after _____."

 *Homework*

An Exciting Trip

Write a story of five or six sentences about a trip you'd like to take. Where would you go? Why would you find it exciting? What would you discover on your trip? Use at least five specific nouns and highlight them. Think of an exciting beginning for your story that will make your reader want to read more. Write a powerful topic sentence and use at least three details or examples to support it. Give your story an original title. Use the space below to plan your story with a brief outline.

_____

_____

_____

_____

_____

_____

_____

_____

_____

Scoring Rubric

1. **Top form (You're a champ!)**	2. **Fair (Keep trying!)**	3. **Needs improvement (Don't give up! You can do it!)**
Composes original title	Composes fairly interesting title	Composes an uninteresting title
Uses five specific nouns	Uses four specific nouns	Uses fewer than four specific nouns
Writes very interesting beginning	Writes interesting beginning	Writes fair-to-poor beginning
Writes excellent topic sentence	Writes good topic sentence	Writes fair-to-poor topic sentence
Supports topic sentence with at least three details	Supports topic sentence with at least three details	Supports topic sentence with fewer than three details
Writes paragraph that has a beginning, middle, and end	Writes paragraph that has a beginning, middle, and end	Writes paragraph that does not have a distinct beginning, middle, and end
Composes original ending	Composes ordinary ending	Composes uninteresting ending
Makes no spelling errors	Makes no more than two spelling errors	More than two spelling errors

Lesson 2: Personal Pronouns

- **Use a pronoun in place of a noun.**

 Think About It: Personal Pronouns

Pronouns are words used in place of nouns. Personal pronouns refer to people. **There are seven personal pronouns: I, you, he, she, it, we, they.** The first five personal pronouns (*I, you, he, she,* and *it*) refer to one person or thing, and they are singular. The last two (*we* and *they*) refer to more than one person, and they are plural. These pronouns are often used as subjects in sentences. Other forms of personal pronouns are **me, him, her, you, it, us, them.** We call these pronouns **object pronouns.**

Another type of personal pronoun, the **possessive pronoun,** shows that somebody owns something. Here are the possessive pronouns: **my, mine, your, yours, his, her, hers, its, our, ours, their, theirs.**

EXAMPLES
1. **Personal Pronoun:** *He* walked the dog at midnight.
2. **Personal Pronoun:** The dog walked *him* at midnight.
3. **Personal Pronoun:** *My* dog howled at midnight and woke the neighbors. (Since the word *my* shows that I own the dog, it is also a possessive pronoun.)

Writing Connection: When we write, we sometimes substitute pronouns for nouns because it sounds better than repeating the noun too many times. Using pronouns can help streamline your writing.

Picture It

Read the story. Highlight the 19 personal pronouns.

Lost in the Mall

My cousin Matt and I went to the mall last weekend. We ate pizza and ice cream at the food court and bought new clothes. After a long day of shopping, we headed out to the parking lot.

Matt shouted to me from across the lot. "I cannot find the car."

I walked over to him. "Maybe that guard can help us."

"What can she do?" asked Matt.

"She can drive us around until we find it," I said.

"That's a good idea. You are a great help to me," said Matt. "I am proud to be your cousin."

Practice

Choose a personal pronoun from the Word Bank to fill in each blank. Score five points for each answer in number 8. Score 10 points for every other answer. Some pronouns are used more than once. **Score** _____

Word Bank					
we	you	us	it	they	I

1. Sean and Malika had planned a trip to the beach. _____ were sorry to see that it was beginning to rain.

2. "What do _____ do now?" asked Sean.

3. "There are a lot of things _____ can still do at the seashore," Malika said.

4. "Do _____ have any ideas?" Sean asked.

5. "My parents said there is a seashell museum, and that we would love _____," Malika said.

6. "If _____ stops raining, we can always go to the beach."

7. "_____ are right," Sean said.

8. "_____ should not let a little rain stop _____ from having a good time."

9. "_____ will pack a picnic lunch," said Malika.

10. "Will _____ bring the snacks and dessert?"

 *Homework*

A Hero for Today

Write a five- to six-sentence essay about a person you would choose as your personal hero. You can write about a famous person or someone you know personally. Give it an original title. Use at least five personal pronouns in your essay and underline them. Highlight the pronouns. Write an outline in the space below.

_____

_____

_____

_____

_____

_____

_____

_____

_____

_____

Scoring Rubric		
1. **Top form (You're a champ!)**	2. **Fair (Keep trying!)**	3. **Needs improvement (Don't give up! You can do it!)**
Composes interesting title	Composes fairly interesting title	Composes an uninteresting title
Uses five personal pronouns	Uses at least four personal pronouns	Uses fewer than four personal pronouns
Writes excellent topic sentence	Writes good topic sentence	Writes fair-to-poor topic sentence
Supports topic sentence with at least three details	Supports topic sentence with at least three details	Supports topic sentence with fewer than three details
Writes paragraph that has a beginning, middle, and end	Writes paragraph that has a beginning, middle, and end	Writes paragraph that does not have a distinct beginning, middle, and end
Makes no spelling errors	Makes no more than two spelling errors	Makes more than two spelling errors

Lesson 3: More Pronouns

- **Interrogative pronouns ask a question.**
- **Demonstrative pronouns point out a specific person, place, or thing.**
- **Indefinite pronouns don't refer to any specific person, place, or thing.**

Think About It

You've learned about personal pronouns. Now let's look at some different types of pronouns. The first type of pronoun, an **interrogative pronoun,** is a pronoun you use to ask a question. There are four interrogative pronouns for you to learn: **who, whose, which,** and **what.** (Actually, there is another, *whom,* but you probably won't use it too often.)

Another type of pronoun is a pronoun that points out a specific person, place, or thing. We call these pronouns **demonstrative pronouns.** Again, you need to learn only four of this type of pronoun: **this, that, these,** and **those.**

The last type of pronoun, the **indefinite pronoun,** doesn't refer to a definite person, place, or thing. You don't need to memorize this list of indefinite pronouns. Just go over them a few times so that you'll recognize them when you see them in sentences.

EXAMPLES: INDEFINITE PRONOUNS			
all	each	most	other
another	either	much	several
any	everybody	neither	some
anybody	everyone	nobody	somebody
anyone	everything	none	someone
anything	few	no one	something
both	many	one	

EXAMPLES: TYPES OF PRONOUNS

1. "*Which* hermit crab would you like?" asked the salesperson. (Interrogative Pronoun)

2. "I'll take the *one* with the orange and yellow shell," said Kim. (Indefinite Pronoun)

3. "I am saving *this* for another customer," said the salesperson. (Demonstrative Pronoun)

4. "Then I will take *another*," Kim said. (Indefinite Pronoun)

Think About It

The four types of pronouns take the place of nouns. If they describe nouns, they are pronouns that act like adjectives (words that describe nouns). Do you remember when linking verbs acted like helping verbs? Before you decide what part of speech a word is, it's a good idea to figure out how it's used in a sentence.

EXAMPLES

Demonstrative Pronoun: *That* is a gigantic tuna sandwich.

Demonstrative Pronoun Used as an Adjective: I can't wait to eat *that* gigantic tuna sandwich.

Indefinite Pronoun: *Both* are baking cakes for Molly's birthday.

Indefinite Pronoun Used as an Adjective: *Both* sisters are baking cakes for Molly's birthday.

Picture It

Read the story. Highlight the 16 pronouns in the story. Label the pronouns with these abbreviations: *POS* for possessive pronouns; *P* for personal pronouns; *INT* for interrogative pronouns (questioning pronouns); *D* for demonstrative pronouns (pronouns that point out); and *I* for indefinite pronouns. Write the code letters above the pronouns.

Music to His Ears

Adam's mother stormed into his room. "What is that horrible loud noise?"

"This is my favorite song, Mom," Adam said.

Mom shook her head. "What are the words to that song? I can't understand any of it."

Mom went to her room and brought back one of her old tapes from the Dark Ages. "This is wonderful music. It is much better than that."

Practice

Choose the best pronoun from the Word Bank to fill in the blanks. Cross off the words as you find them. Two words are used twice. Score 10 points for each correct answer. **Score** _____

Word Bank			
everyone	who	you	every
my	all	me	I

1. _____ student in my class attended the pep rally.

2. _____ of the football players ran out on the field.

3. The cheerleaders led _____ in cheers.

4. _____ voice was hoarse from shouting the cheers.

5. "_____ sounds like a frog?" my teacher asked.

6. I could see everybody looking at _____.

7. "Are you looking at _____?" I asked the boy next to me.

8. "I am looking at _____," he said.

9. "Do _____ think I sound like a frog, too?"

10. "No. _____ was just thinking about how I'd like to know you better," he said.

 ## Homework

My Favorite School Subject

Write a six- to eight-sentence essay about your favorite school subject, using at least three different types of pronouns. Highlight the pronouns and label them using the code below.

Include this information in your essay: Why do you like the subject? What kinds of careers does your favorite subject include? Here are the types of pronouns you can choose from: Personal (P), Possessive (POS), Interrogative (questioning) (INT), Demonstrative (pronouns that point out) (D), and Indefinite (pronouns that don't refer to any specific person, place, or thing) (I). Write your outline in the space below.

_____

_____

_____

_____

_____

_____

_____

_____

_____

_____

_____

_____

_____

_____

Warm-up: Nouns and Pronouns

- **Common nouns name any person, place, thing, or idea.**
- **Proper nouns name specific persons, places, things, or ideas.**
- **Capitalize proper nouns.**
- **Singular nouns tell about one person, place, thing, or idea.**
- **Plural nouns tell about more than one person, place, thing, or idea.**
- **Pronouns take the place of nouns.**
- **Pronouns can also describe nouns.**
- **Possessive pronouns show that someone owns something.**
- **Pronouns can be used as subjects or objects of a sentence.**
- **Interrogative pronouns ask a question.**
- **Demonstrative pronouns point out specific persons, places, or things.**
- **Indefinite pronouns don't refer to specific persons, places, or things.**

Relay Race

Use the clues in each of the sentences on the next page to answer the riddles about nouns and pronouns. Write your answers in the blank spaces, using words from the Word Bank. Check off the words in the Word Bank as you write your answers. Score 10 points for each correct answer. **Score** _____

Word Bank			
indefinite	pronoun	demonstrative	common noun
plural	possessive	interrogative pronoun	
capital	singular	describe	

1. When you don't want to repeat the nouns in your sentence, you can depend on me to help. _____

2. Do you want to ask a question? Don't hesitate. I'm always around.

   _____

3. I'm a pronoun, and I can wear two hats. Sometimes I take the place of nouns, but sometimes I _____ nouns.

4. I'm not wishy-washy, but I don't like talking about specific persons or things. What kind of pronoun am I? _____

5. I'm a prim and proper noun. That's why I always begin with this type of letter. _____

6. I only like to talk about one person, place, thing, or idea at a time. Don't bother me with numbers. What kind of noun am I?

   _____

7. Four words belong to my family, and I'm always pointing out things. What type of pronoun am I? _____

8. I'm not fussy. I talk about any person, place, thing, or idea. Who am I?

   _____

9. I name more than one person, place, thing, or idea. Thinking about just one bores me. I'm a _____ noun.

10. I'm greedy. I like to own everything I can. And I don't like to share. Call me a _____ pronoun.

Describe Powerfully with Adjectives

Lesson 1: Descriptive Adjectives, Articles, and Predicate Adjectives

- **Adjectives describe nouns and pronouns.**

💡 *Think About It*

Descriptive adjectives describe nouns and pronouns. Three adjectives (*a, an,* and *the*) also describe nouns. We call them **articles.**

EXAMPLES: DESCRIPTIVE ADJECTIVES

1. My friends crowded around my brother when he drove his *red* convertible to school. (*Red* describes *car.*)
2. The *shaggy* dog slobbered all over me. (*Shaggy* describes *dog.*)

EXAMPLES: ARTICLES

1. *The* bridge opened to let *the tall* ships pass. *The* (article) describes *bridge.* *The* (article) and *tall* (descriptive adjective) describe *ships.*
2. *An old* trolley took the wedding party to the reception. *An* (article) and *old* (descriptive adjective) describe *trolley.*

Predicate adjectives come after linking verbs. They describe the subject, the main word in a sentence.

EXAMPLE

The red and gold leaves look *brilliant* in the fall. *Brilliant* (predicate adjective) describes the noun, *leaves.* Can you find and name the other adjectives in this sentence?

Pronouns can also act as adjectives when they describe nouns.

> **EXAMPLE**
>
> *That* movie gave me goose bumps. *That* (pronoun used as an adjective) describes the noun, *movie.*

Nouns can act as adjectives, too.

> **EXAMPLE**
>
> The *monster* storm closed in on our vacation cottage. *Monster* is a noun, but here it acts as an adjective because it describes another noun, *storm.*

Some nouns that act as adjectives are very closely related to the nouns they describe. We call these **compound nouns** (*soap opera, home plate, goose bumps*).

 Writing Connection: Adjectives can make your descriptions of nouns and pronouns more lively. Try to use specific adjectives to describe what you're writing about. General adjectives that don't carry a punch will bore your reader.

> **EXAMPLES**
>
> **General adjectives:** The *awesome* play was so *great* that we couldn't stop clapping.
> **Specific adjectives:** The *lively* actors and actresses and the *soulful* music made the school play a *rousing* success.

Picture It

Read the story below. Highlight the 29 adjectives. Write *D* above descriptive adjectives, *A* above articles, and *PA* above predicate adjectives. Write *Pro* above the pronouns used as adjectives. Write *N* above nouns used as adjectives.

Rock Concert Madness

A long line of cars wrapped around the winding road leading to the expressway exit. Would we make it to the rock concert on time? My sister and I were worried. The cars in front of us started  honking. The big concert would begin in ten minutes. Finally, the cars started moving. My sister parked her shiny car in an underground garage. We raced up the steep steps to the beautiful new building. We settled into the comfortable, leather seats and sat back to enjoy the rock star's powerful voice.

Practice

Choose an adjective from the Word Bank to fill in each blank. Use each answer once. Write the type of adjective used above the adjective in the sentence. Use these abbreviations: *D*, descriptive; *A*, article; *PA*, predicate adjective; *PRO*, pronoun used as adjective; *NA*, noun used as adjective. Score five points for each correct adjective and five points for naming the type of adjective. **Score** _____

Word Bank				
that	strange	baked	grilled	grated
school	angry	long	vegetable	favorite

1. My friend and I walked up to the _____ lunch line.

2. The cafeteria worker smiled at us. "Do you want hot dogs and _____ beans or chipped beef?" he asked.

3. "I would rather have _____ hamburgers or a crispy salad," I said.

4. "I can give you a _____ platter with spinach, broccoli, and cauliflower," he said.

5. "I would rather have a bowl of spaghetti and meatballs with _____ cheese," my friend said.

6. I could tell that the tall boy in back of me was _____.

7. "I have been waiting a _____ time."

8. "My stomach is making _____ gurgling noises," the tall boy said.

9. At _____ moment my mom came running into the cafeteria with a big, brown bag.

10. "I made your _____ lunch, a peanut butter and marshmallow sandwich," she said. "I read the menu in the paper, and I knew you wouldn't like the school lunch!"

 ## *Homework*

A Natural Wonder

Write a paragraph of six to eight sentences about something beautiful you've observed in nature. Use at least four vivid, descriptive adjectives, and underline them. Think of colorful, specific adjectives that will make your reader *see* what you're trying to say. Before you write, make your notes here.

_____

_____

_____

_____

_____

_____

_____

_____

_____

_____

_____

_____

Scoring Rubric		
1. **Top form (You're a champ!)**	2. **Fair (Keep trying!)**	3. **Needs improvement (Don't give up! You can do it!)**
Composes interesting title	Composes interesting title	Composes an uninteresting title
Uses four vivid descriptive adjectives	Uses at least three vivid descriptive adjectives	Uses fewer than three vivid descriptive adjectives
Writes excellent topic sentence	Writes good topic sentence	Writes fair-to-poor topic sentence
Supports topic sentence with at least four details	Supports topic sentence with at least four details	Supports topic sentence with fewer than four details
Writes paragraph that has a beginning, middle, and end	Writes paragraph that has a beginning, middle, and end	Writes paragraph that does not have a distinct beginning, middle, and end
Makes no spelling errors	Makes no more than one spelling error	Makes two or more spelling errors

Lesson 2: How Adjectives Compare

- **Adjectives help compare nouns and pronouns.**

Think About It

Besides describing nouns and pronouns, adjectives also help us compare one noun to another.

EXAMPLES
Pinocchio had a *big* nose.   When Pinocchio lied, he grew a *bigger* nose.   When he told a huge lie, Pinocchio grew the *biggest* nose in the world.

The **positive degree** of an adjective (*big, exciting*) is the first level of comparison. When we want to say something is stronger than the first level, we go to the **comparative degree** (*bigger, easier*). When we want to say we can't go higher than this, we've reached the **superlative degree** of comparing nouns (*biggest, easiest*). You can't top the superlative degree. You can remember that it is the highest level of comparison because *super* gives you the idea of being the best.

To form the comparative and superlative of one-syllable words, add *er* and *est*.

EXAMPLE
strong, stronger, strongest

Some adjectives that have two syllables form their comparative and superlative degrees by adding *er* or *est*.

EXAMPLE
happy, happier, happiest

Other adjectives of two syllables use *more* and *most* to form their comparative and superlative degrees.

EXAMPLE
careful, more careful, most careful

You'll need to think a little harder with some other adjectives. These adjectives form completely different words in the comparative and superlative degrees. Here are some common ones: *bad, worse, worst; much, more, most;* and *good, better, best.*

Think About It: Using Degrees of Comparison

We use the comparative degree to compare two things. We use the superlative degree to compare more than two things.

EXAMPLES
1. Burger Heaven was the *better* of the two restaurants.
2. The Ferris wheel at Wonderland was the *best* I've ever ridden.

Picture It

State whether the *italicized* adjectives are in the positive (P), comparative (C), or superlative (S) degree. Write your answer above the adjective.

Little Green Men

"Look," said Chris, pointing to the *bright* light in the sky.

"That *big* object looks like a UFO." As it came closer, Jay and Chris saw that the *strange* object was *larger* than they had thought.

"That is the *most unusual* thing I've ever seen," said Chris.

"The lights are *brighter* than the sun, and I think I see *tiny* windows on the side of it."

"Do you see *little* green men peeking out, too?" asked Jay.

"No, but I'm not staying here to find out," Chris said as he raced toward home.

Practice

In the space after the words, write whether the adjectives in *italics* are in the positive, comparative or superlative degree. Use the abbreviations *P* (positive), *C* (comparative), and *S* (superlative). Score 10 points for each correct answer.
Score _____

1. *tinier* baby _____
2. *clean* room _____
3. *more cautious* driver _____
4. *fastest* car _____
5. *longer* caterpillar _____
6. *most punctual* student _____
7. *worst* food _____
8. *patient* teacher _____
9. *most beautiful* sunrise _____
10. *good* candy _____

Homework

Using the adjectives below, fill in the chart to write the three degrees of comparison. Use a dictionary to check your answers. Score 10 points for each correct answer. **Score** _____

1. *simple* problem 2. *long* movie 3. *cheerful* grandmother 4. *proud* parent
5. *cute* kitten 6. *healthy* food 7. *hard* test 8. *funny* puppy 9. *high* kite
10. *good* dessert

Positive	Comparative	Superlative

Warm-up: Adjectives

- **Adjectives describe nouns or pronouns.**
- **The three articles (*a*, *an*, and *the*) also describe nouns and pronouns.**
- **Other parts of speech, like pronouns and nouns, act as adjectives when they describe nouns.**
- **Predicate adjectives come after linking verbs and describe nouns and pronouns.**
- **Use positive, comparative, and superlative degrees to show how little or how much an adjective compares something.**

Relay Race

Part 1: In the space after each sentence, write how the adjective in *italics* is used. Use these abbreviations: *D*, descriptive; *A*, article; *PA*, predicate adjective; *PRO*, pronoun used as adjective; *NA*, noun used as an adjective. Score 10 points for each correct answer. **Score** _____

1. Carly found a *colorful* butterfly beneath the cherry tree in her backyard.

   _____

2. "I would love to show my science teacher *that* butterfly," she told her friend Dylan.

   _____

3. "It is the most *beautiful* butterfly I've ever seen," said Dylan. _____

4. "It has *rainbow* colors that gleam in the sun," said Carly. _____

5. "Butterflies live only a *short* time," said Dylan. "Why not set it free?" _____

6. "That is a good idea," Carly said, as she gave back the *fluttering* insect to the sky.

   _____

Part 2: Tell whether the adjectives are in the positive (*P*), comparative (*C*), or superlative (*S*) degree. Write your answer in the space after the sentence. Score 10 points for each correct answer. **Score** _____

7. When Carly got home, she painted a picture of the *most amazing* butterfly she'd ever seen. _____

8. She remembered the *tiny* splashes of color and drew them from memory.

   _____

9. As she grew *more tired*, she wondered if she'd complete her painting. _____

10. She took a *short* rest and then went back to work. Her science teacher would see the butterfly, after all. _____

Advance the Action with Adverbs

Lesson 1: Adverbs Tell About Verbs, Adjectives, and Other Adverbs

- **An adverb modifies a verb, an adjective, or another adverb.**

Think About It

You've learned that adjectives describe nouns and pronouns. Adverbs are describing words, too. They describe verbs, adjectives, and other adverbs. **Adverbs** tell how, when, where, why, how often, and how much.

EXAMPLES

Adverbs Describing Verbs:

Adam throws the ball *forcefully*. (how)

Sarah will go to the mall *later*. (when)

A noisy ghost lives *here*. (where)

Pablo goes to hockey games *often*. (how much)

Adverbs Describing Adjectives:

My teacher's voice is *really* loud when she gets angry. (The adverb *really* modifies the predicate adjective *loud*. It tells how much.)

Adverb Describing Other Adverbs:

The balloons burst *very* loudly. (The adverb *very* modifies the adverb *loudly*.)

Picture It

Highlight the *italicized* adverbs in the story. Use this code to label the adverbs: AV (adverb modifying verb), AAD (adverb modifying adjective), AADV (adverb modifying other adverb).

A Trip to the Rain Forest

Caitlin and Shane had *always* wanted to see the rain forest movie at the science museum.

One day their foster mother said, "I have *very* good news for you. We are *finally* going to see the show on that *amazingly* big screen at the museum."

When Caitlin and Shane arrived *there*, they sat in seats surrounding the stage. The screen was so big that it took up the whole wall. *Soon*, the movie began. Caitlin and Shane thought they were *actually* part of the movie as the scientists climbed the tall trees to learn about the rain forest. They could *practically* touch the monkeys in the trees.

Suddenly, Shane felt very dizzy and sick to his stomach. The room seemed to be spinning *wildly*. When the show ended, the audience clapped *very loudly*.

"I *really* enjoyed the show," Caitlin said to her foster mother.

"Yes, but the next time we go to the museum show remind me not to eat nachos, cheddar fries, and cherry pie. Maybe *then* I won't feel *so* sick," Shane said, bolting *quickly* from the theater.

Think About It

Sometimes nouns can be used as adverbs, too.

EXAMPLE
My friend from Mexico arrived yesterday. (The noun *yesterday* modifies the verb *arrived*, so it's an adverb.)

Practice

In the space after each sentence, explain how each *italicized* word is used. Use these codes to answer: AV (adverb modifying a verb); AAD (adverb modifying an adjective); NA (noun used as an adverb); AADV (adverb modifying another adverb). Score 10 points for each correct answer. **Score** _____

1. Tamika saw that it was a *very* rainy holiday. _____

2. "What can we do *today*?" she asked her sister Missy. _____

3. "Why don't we arrange some of these family pictures in albums? We could do it *very* quickly and still have time to watch our soap operas," Missy said.
_____

4. "I've *always* wanted to organize these pictures, but I've never had time," Tamika said. _____

5. Missy *quickly* gathered the old shoe boxes filled with family pictures.
_____

6. After they had spent time laughing at their baby pictures, the sisters *finally* finished their job. _____

7. Mom and Dad got home *late* from work. _____

8. "What did you do *today*?" asked Dad. "What a rainy holiday!"
_____

9. "We worked *hard*, but we had fun," Tamika said, showing their parents the albums they had filled. _____

10. "We had *so* much fun that we forgot all about our soap operas," said Missy.
_____

Homework

Something Scary

Write a six- to eight-sentence friendly letter about something scary that happened to you or a friend. (If you can't think of anything, make up a story.) Use at least four adverbs and highlight them. Use the space below for notes.

_____

_____

_____

_____

_____

_____

_____

_____

_____

_____

_____

_____

Scoring Rubric

1. Top form (You're a champ!)	2. Fair (Keep trying!)	3. Needs improvement (Don't give up! You can do it!)
Uses correct letter form	Uses correct letter form	Uses incorrect letter form
Uses at least four adverbs	Uses at least three adverbs	Uses fewer than three adverbs
States main idea clearly	States main idea fairly clearly	States main idea unclearly
Supports main idea with at least four details	Supports main idea with at least four details	Supports main idea with fewer than four details
Writes letter that has a beginning, middle, and end	Writes letter that has a beginning, middle, and end	Writes letter that does not have a distinct beginning, middle, and end
Makes no spelling errors	Makes no more than two spelling errors	Makes more than two spelling errors

Lesson 2: How Adverbs Compare

- **Use the positive, comparative, and superlative degrees to compare how much or how little an adverb compares something.**

Think About It

Just as you did with adjectives, you can use positive, comparative, and superlative degrees to show how much or how little an adverb compares something. The positive degree is the first level of comparison. It's the adverb in its basic form. The **positive degree** tells about a verb, an adjective, or another adverb without comparing it to anything or anyone else.

> **EXAMPLE**
>
> The fireman acted *quickly*.

Just like the comparative degree with adjectives, the comparative degree is the second level of comparison. The **comparative degree** of an adverb compares two persons, places, things, or ideas.

> **EXAMPLE**
>
> The fireman acted *more quickly* than the bystander.

The superlative degree is the third and final level of comparison. The **superlative degree** of an adverb compares three or more persons, places, things, or ideas.

> **EXAMPLE**
>
> The fire chief acted the *most quickly* of all the people on the scene.

As with adjectives, many one-syllable adverbs form the comparative and superlative degrees by adding *er* and *est* (*soon, sooner, soonest*). While some adjectives having more than one syllable add *er* or *est* to form the comparative and superlative degrees, many adverbs use *more* and *most* to form these degrees (*often, more often, most often.*)

Using your common sense will help you figure out the comparative and superlative degrees of adverbs and adjectives. It would sound strange to say *oftener* and *oftenest*, wouldn't it? When in doubt, use your dictionary.

Picture It

Highlight the adverbs in the positive degree. Circle the adverbs in the comparative degree. All of the adverbs are written in *italics*.

Cry Baby

I thought that baby-sitting my neighbor's baby would be the easiest job in the world. He had slept *peacefully* all afternoon. After dinner he began crying *softly*, so I picked him up. When he cried *louder* and kicked his feet, I tried to comfort him by singing him a song. That didn't work, so I *calmly* read him a story. He kept crying and kicked his feet even *harder*. Would he ever calm down? I felt like crying myself.

Then I had an idea. I started crying *loudly*. Then the baby started giggling and moving his arms *wildly*. After that I sang him another song and read him another story. But this time the baby smiled *more calmly* and then fell asleep. I have to say it was the most fun I'd ever had baby-sitting even though the day had started off *poorly*.

Practice

In the space after each of the following sentences, identify the *italicized* adverbs as positive (P), comparative (C), or superlative (S). Score 10 points for each correct answer. **Score** _____

1. Ms. Hernandez speaks Spanish *better* than her students do. _____

2. A gazelle runs *fast*. _____

3. Darrel ate the candy bars *quickly*. _____

4. Tyler wrote the *most exciting* story. _____

5. Tracy's cat is *more stubborn* than her dog. _____

6. Abe sings the high notes *well*. _____

7. My math teacher *frequently* gives pop quizzes. _____

8. Courtney spoke the *loudest* when she gave her speech. _____

9. Raheem *patiently* explained the math problem to his friend. _____

10. Erin moved *more slowly* than a caterpillar. _____

Homework

My Happiest Moment

Write a six- to eight-sentence paragraph about one of your happiest moments. In your paragraph, use one adverb in each of the three different degrees: positive (P), comparative (C), and superlative (S). Underline the adverbs and label them using the codes. Think of an original title for your story. Make your outline in this space.

_____

_____

_____

_____

_____

_____

_____

_____

_____

_____

_____

_____

_____

_____

_____

_____

Warm-up: Adverbs

- **Adverbs describe verbs, adjectives, and other adverbs.**
- **Adverbs tell how, when, where, why, how often, and how much.**
- **Nouns sometimes act as adverbs when they describe verbs.**
- **Use positive, comparative, and superlative degrees to show how little or how much an adverb compares something.**

Relay Race

Score 10 points for each correct answer. **Score** _____

Part 1: Use the code to tell whether the adverbs in *italics* describe a verb (V), adjective (ADJ), or another adverb (ADV).

1. The teacher looked *very* grumpy when I asked her for the third time to explain adverbs. _____

2. "Don't you *ever* pay attention?" she asked. _____

3. "Of course I do," I answered *very* quickly since fire was coming out of her ears. _____

4. She sighed and looked at me *more* calmly. "Then why did you ask that question?" _____

5. "I guess I've been thinking a lot about baseball *lately*. You have to admit. It's a lot more exciting than adverbs." _____

Part 2: Tell whether the adverbs in *italics* tell how, when, where, why, how often, or how much. Write your answers in the space after each sentence.

6. Alyssa will apply for a job in a pet store *tomorrow*. _____

7. If she gets the job, she will go *there* right away. _____

8. She will be *very* happy if she gets the job. _____

Part 3: Tell whether the adverbs in italics are in the positive (P), comparative (C), or superlative (S) degree.

9. Lew plays the trumpet *better* than anyone I know. _____

10. Sandra answered questions the most *intelligently* of all the students when she was interviewed for the job. _____

Press On with Prepositions

Lesson 1: Prepositions Show Relationships

- **A preposition shows the relationship of its object (a noun or a pronoun) to another word in the sentence.**

Think About It

Preposition is a big word for a lot of little words that are easy to learn. Prepositions give you another way to make your sentences more descriptive and interesting. Just as adjectives and adverbs describe other words in the sentence, prepositional phrases add meat to a sentence's bare bones.

EXAMPLES

1. The playful puppy ran around the classroom. In this sentence, the preposition *around* shows the relationship between the verb *ran* and the noun *classroom*.

2. The e-mail from my friend was interesting. In this sentence, the preposition *from* shows the relationship between the noun *e-mail* and the noun *friend*.

LIST OF PREPOSITIONS

Become familiar with this list of commonly used prepositions. Using them in sentences will help you recognize them.

about	before	during	of	to
above	behind	except	off	toward
across	below	for	on	under
after	beneath	from	out	until
against	beside	in	over	up
along	between	inside	past	upon
among	beyond	into	since	with
around	by	like	through	within
at	down	near	throughout	without

💡 *Think About It*

The group of words starting with a preposition and ending with a noun is called a **prepositional phrase.** Just as an adjective describes or modifies a noun or pronoun, a prepositional phrase can describe a noun or a pronoun.

A prepositional phrase must begin with a preposition and end with a noun or a pronoun. We call the noun or pronoun that ends the phrase the **object of the preposition.** There can never be a verb in a prepositional phrase.

EXAMPLES: PREPOSITIONAL PHRASES THAT DESCRIBE A NOUN OR PRONOUN
1. The boy with the milk mustache asked Annie to the dance. (The prepositional phrase *with the milk mustache* describes the noun *boy*. It acts like an adjective because it modifies a noun.)
2. The ferret across the street escaped from its cage. (The prepositional phrase *across the street* describes the noun *ferret*. It acts like an adjective because it modifies a noun.)

EXAMPLES: PREPOSITIONAL PHRASES THAT DESCRIBE A VERB
1. Aaron parasailed over the ocean. (The prepositional phrase *over the ocean* modifies the verb *parasailed*. It acts like an adverb because it modifies a verb.)
2. Lori sat behind the class clown. (The prepositional phrase *behind the class clown* modifies the verb *sat*. It acts like an adverb because it modifies a verb.)

📷 *Picture It*

Highlight the prepositional phrases. All of the prepositional phrases are in *italics*. Label the adjective phrases ADJ and the adverb phrases ADV.

A Sweet Offer

I live *beside the corner store*. Pop Thomas, the owner, keeps fifty different types *of penny candy inside a glass case*. Every time I buy groceries there, he lets me choose a few pieces *of candy from the case*. Sometimes I help *with the customers*.

Yesterday Pop Thomas offered me a job *in his store*. I told him I could work *from afternoon until night on the weekends*. He said that he would talk *to me about the job* tomorrow. I can hardly wait.

Practice

Choose the best preposition from the Word Bank to begin each prepositional phrase. (Use one word twice.) Write your answers in the space provided. Score 10 points for each correct answer. **Score** _____

Word Bank				
under	into	of	after	among
with	at	in	inside	

1. My big chance to perform in front _____ an audience was about to begin.

2. I looked _____ the crowd waiting for me to sing with the karaoke machine.

3. I trembled with fear as I looked at my friends sitting _____ the audience.

4. The audience pounded on the tables _____ their fists and shouted, "We want Jamal. We want Jamal."

5. My music teacher brought me a glass _____ water. My best friend Willie wiped my head with a bandana.

6. The music started. I told myself that I was _____ friends and had nothing to fear.

7. I heard myself singing loudly _____ the microphone.

8. My knees were knocking _____ my slacks, but I kept singing.

9. I heard myself hit a sour note, and I felt like crawling _____ the stage.

10. _____ the show, everyone told me they never knew I could sing like that. And nobody mentioned the sour note.

Writing Connection: Paragraphing

You've had a lot of experience writing one paragraph. Now you're ready to move on to writing two paragraphs. Writing more than one paragraph is easy if you keep a few basics in mind:

1. Each new paragraph needs its own topic sentence. 2.Back up each topic sentence with supporting details as you did when you wrote one paragraph. 3. Give each paragraph a closing sentence that summarizes what the paragraph is about.

 *Homework*

A Dream Job

Write two paragraphs of five to eight sentences each about a job you'd love to have. Use at least four prepositional phrases. Circle the prepositions and highlight the prepositional phrases. Remember that *a prepositional phrase must have a preposition and an object*. It may also have other words like adjectives, but it never has a verb. Plan your essay in this space.

_____

_____

_____

_____

_____

_____

_____

_____

_____

_____

_____

_____

_____

_____

_____

_____

_____

_____

Lesson 2: Pronoun Case After Prepositions

- **Use object pronouns after prepositions.**

Think About It

Object pronouns show up in one of two ways in a sentence. You will see them after action verbs or as the last word in a prepositional phrase. The pronouns *me*, *you*, *him*, *her*, *it*, *us*, and *them* are used as objects of prepositions.

EXAMPLES: PRONOUNS USED AS OBJECTS OF THE PREPOSITION

1. Would you like to go bungee jumping with Raymond and *me?*

2. The Bulldog bared its teeth at Raj and *me.*

Do these sentences sound correct to you? If they sound incorrect, it's probably because you're used to hearing the wrong forms of pronouns after prepositions. Always use an object pronoun after a preposition. If you're not sure of which pronoun to use, read the sentence, leaving out the first object. Then it will be easy to see the right answer.

In the first example, if you left out *Raymond and*, you would complete the sentence with the word *me*. Try reading it with *I*: *Would you like to go bungee jumping with I?* Does that sound correct to you? If not, how would you correct it?

Picture It

In each sentence below, circle the pronoun in *italics* when it is used correctly as an object of the preposition. Put a slash mark (/) over the incorrect pronouns.

1. The picture of my principal in the pie-eating contest was taken by Cassandra and *me*.
2. Students like Bernard and *he* get detention every day.
3. Would you please give directions to me and *her?*
4. The teacher is always looking at you and *I*.
5. Would you like to go to the wax museum with Sujatha and *me?*
6. I made chocolate covered ants for my cousin and *he*.
7. A giant spider sat between my brother and *me*.
8. Shall we go to the sports banquet with the coach and *her?*

Practice

If the object pronouns in *italics* are correct, write *C* in the space provided. If they are incorrect, write *I*. Score 10 points for each correct answer. **Score** _____

1. The hippopotamus ran after Shelly and *I*. _____
2. A big, grizzly bear wanted a treat from my friends and *me*. _____
3. Would you like to have a picnic lunch with my mother and *he?* _____
4. I'd like to take a walk with you and *them*. _____
5. After the class trip, I'll go home with your mother and *him*. _____
6. Look at the big iguana near Jasmine and *she*. _____
7. Twins like Jesse and *he* usually get along very well. _____
8. The trip was fun for my friend and *me*. _____
9. The teacher said she could depend on Amy and *her*. _____
10. Please send the pictures of the trip to my friend and *I*. _____

Homework

Letter to the Editor: An Important Issue

Write a two-paragraph letter to the editor of your school or local newspaper about an issue that is important to you. Use at least three pairs of object pronouns after prepositions. Highlight the object pronouns. Underline the prepositional phrases. Make your outline here.

_____

_____

_____

_____

_____

_____

_____

_____

_____

_____

_____

_____

_____

_____

_____

_____

_____

_____

Warm-up: Parts of Speech: Verbs, Nouns, Pronouns, Adjectives, Adverbs, Prepositions

- **Action verbs show action you create with your body or your mind.**
- **Linking verbs link the subject to another word in a sentence.**
- **Helping verbs work with main verbs.**
- **Nouns name persons, places, things, or ideas.**
- **Pronouns take the place of nouns.**
- **Adjectives describe nouns or pronouns.**
- **The articles *a*, *an*, and *the* describe nouns and pronouns.**
- **Predicate adjectives come after linking verbs. They describe nouns and pronouns.**
- **Adverbs describe verbs, adjectives, and other adverbs.**
- **Adverbs tell how, when, where, why, how often, and how much.**
- **A preposition shows the relationship of a noun or a pronoun to another word in a sentence.**
- **A prepositional phrase begins with a preposition and ends with a noun.**
- **The pronouns *me*, *you*, *him*, *her*, *it*, *us*, and *them* are used as objects of prepositions. They are also called object pronouns.**

Relay Race

Part 1: Identify the parts of speech in *italics* on the line after each sentence. All of the parts of speech are in the Word Bank. Some parts of speech are used more than once. **Hint:** Think about how the word is used in the sentence before deciding on your answer. Score four points for each correct answer. **Score** _____

Word Bank			
article	noun	action verb	pronoun
adjective	preposition	linking verb	predicate adjective
adverb	helping verb		

1. Jade and her friend Denzell threw a *surprise* birthday party for their best friend Leon. _____

2. They worked *hard* to make it a special day. _____

3. Jade and Denzell *baked* cakes and cookies the night before the party. _____

4. The day *of* the party everyone gathered in Leon's basement. _____

5. Jade asked *everyone* to be very quiet until Leon, the guest of honor, returned home. _____

6. Denzell peeked *through* the curtain to see if Leon was coming. _____

7. Everyone heard *Leon's* dog Bozo barking loudly as Leon got closer to the house. _____

8. "Surprise!" everyone shouted. Leon put his hands on his face. "What *is* going on?" he asked. _____

9. "*Were* you really surprised?" Jade asked. _____

10. "I never suspected," Leon said. "This is *amazing*." _____

11. "Let's eat," Denzell said. "*Then* we can go outside and play games." _____

12. Leon followed his friends to the picnic *table*. _____

13. "What happened to *the* chicken?" Denzell shouted. "I left it right here." _____

14. "Oh, no," *Leon* said. _____

15. "Look over there. My dog Bozo *is* celebrating my birthday, too. He must love your cooking." _____

16. "Well, at least we still have potato salad and dessert," Denzell said, patting Bozo on *his* head. _____

17. After *they* ate, everyone played baseball and touch football. _____

18. Bozo *chased* them around the yard. _____

19. "*Now* it's time for cake," Denzell said. _____

20. All the guests ate cake until it came out of their ears. Even *Bozo* had a piece and begged for more. _____

Part 2: Choose the correct objective case pronoun to complete each sentence. Write your answer in the space provided. Score four points for each correct answer. **Score** _____

21. I have been friends with Jason and (him, he) since kindergarten. _____

22. Would you go to the movies with Ryan and (me, I)? _____

23. The teacher relies on Eduardo and (she, her) for the answers. _____

24. Sisters like Terry and (me, I) will be friends forever. _____

25. The CD player belongs to Luis and (they, them). _____

Make Sense with Sentences

Lesson 1: Parts of a Simple Sentence

- **A simple sentence has a subject and a predicate and expresses a complete thought.**

Think About It

By this time, you can easily pick out nouns, pronouns, and verbs from a sentence. You understand how each part of speech works. Now you're going to learn how to use these different parts of speech in sentences. One main ingredient of a sentence is the action word or verb. We call a verb the **predicate** when we're talking about parts of a sentence.

It's easy to find the predicate in a sentence. Just look for the word that expresses physical or mental action. Sometimes the predicate can be a linking verb (part of the verb *to be*, like *am* or *is*).

Once you find the predicate in a sentence, you can look for the subject. The **subject** of a sentence tells who or what the sentence is about. All you have to do to find the subject is to ask *who* or *what* before the predicate.

You will learn about three different types of sentences. The easiest type to write is a **simple sentence.** It's called a simple sentence because it has only one main thought. A simple sentence must have at least a subject and a predicate. Sometimes it has adjectives, adverbs, and prepositional phrases. The most important thing to remember is that a sentence always expresses a complete thought.

EXAMPLES: SUBJECTS AND PREDICATES IN A SIMPLE SENTENCE

1. Antonio walloped his opponent.

Predicate: walloped

Ask *who* or *what* to find the subject: Who walloped? *Antonio* walloped.

Antonio is the subject of the sentence.

2. Emily found her guinea pig under her bed.

Predicate: found

Ask *who* or *what* to find the subject: Who found? *Emily* found.

Emily is the subject of the sentence.

Think About It: Subject Pronouns

In Unit 2, you learned that the pronouns *I, you, he, she, it, we,* and *they* are subject pronouns. Like nouns, they can be subjects of sentences.

EXAMPLE

He jumped up when he heard the fire alarm go off.

Predicate: jumped

Ask *who* or *what* to find the subject: Who jumped? *He* jumped.

The pronoun *he* is the subject of the sentence.

Think About It

Sometimes the subject of a sentence is invisible. You can't see it, but it's there. In fact, a sentence can be just one little word.

EXAMPLE: *HOP!*

If you ask who hops, you get the answer *you*. This sentence is a command telling *you* to hop. When we can't see the subject of a sentence, we call it *you understood*. *You* is the subject of command sentences even though we can't see it.

MORE EXAMPLES

1. Leave!

Predicate: Leave

Ask *who* or *what* to find the subject: Who leaves? *You* leave.

You is the subject of the sentence.

2. Smile.

Predicate: Smile

Ask *who* or *what* to find the subject: Who smiles? *You* smile.

You is the subject of the sentence.

Think About It: The Direct Object

In Unit 5, you learned about the object of the preposition. There's another part of a sentence called the direct object. The direct object is a noun or a pronoun that receives the action of the verb and shows the result of the action.

You'll find direct objects in some, but not all, sentences. You can find the direct object of a sentence by asking *whom* or *what* after the predicate. Direct objects follow action verbs but never follow linking verbs.

EXAMPLES

1. The sloppy student slurped his soda.
Predicate: slurped
Ask *whom* or *what* to find the object: Slurped what?
Answer: soda
Soda is the direct object of the sentence.

2. Rob asked Dad for an advance on his allowance.
Predicate: asked
Ask *whom* or *what* to find the object: Asked whom?
Answer: Dad
Dad is the direct object of the sentence.

Think About It: Object Pronouns

The object pronouns that you used as objects of the preposition are the pronouns you will use as direct objects following an action verb. They are *me, you, him, her, it, us,* and *them.*

When using two objects for one verb, you may have to think about it more, just as you did with prepositions that had two objects. You can try out each pronoun separately to see what fits best, just as you did with double objects of the preposition.

EXAMPLES

1. The teacher asked Ricardo and me to clap erasers.
Predicate: asked
Ask *whom* or *what* to find the object: Asked whom? Answer: Ricardo and me
Ricardo and *Me* are the direct objects of the sentence.

2. My dad asked her and me for a ride on our new scooter.
Predicate: asked
Ask *whom* or *what* to find the object: Asked whom? Answer: her and me
Her and *me* are the direct objects of the sentence.

Picture It

Read the story and tell whether the words in *italics* are subjects (S), predicates (P), or objects (O). Write the code for the correct part of the sentence in the space at the end of each sentence.

The Meeting

Angel was all alone. _____ She had just *started* school in a new neighborhood. _____ The students there had their own *friends*. _____ She *told* her parents that she wanted to go back to her old school. _____ "*We* must stay here," they said. _____ "Our new *jobs* are here." _____

One day her teacher asked *her* if she wanted to go to a meeting after school. _____ "I don't *know* anyone," Angel said. _____

"They don't know *you*, either," the teacher said _____. "*You* will get to know each other." _____

Angel *went* to the meeting. _____ The *students* were talking and laughing _____. "Who are those presents for?" Angel asked, looking at the pile of wrapped gifts on the table.

"*They* are for children in the orphanage," Jon said._____ "We need *help*. _____ Would you like to help us?"

"Sure," Angel *said*. _____ Everyone worked until they had wrapped all the *presents*. _____ Then *they* went to the diner for something to eat.

_____

Practice

Label the words in *italics* as subjects (S), predicates (P), or objects (O). Write your answer in the space following each sentence. Score 10 points for each correct answer. **Score** _____

1. The students in Ms. Jackson's class were having a *debate.* _____

2. "I *like* the city best," Corey said. _____

3. "I like the country," said Amber. "My *grandmother* lives there." _____

4. "They *have* a farm with horses, cows, and chickens." _____

5. "*I* can go anywhere without a car in the city," Justin said. "I just hop on the bus." _____

6. Sevasti raised her *hand.* "But you see more flowers in the country. You can walk on the grass instead of the sidewalk." _____

7. "There is more to do in the city," Rosa said. "I *go* to games, plays, and concerts all the time." _____

8. "I can't decide which is best," said Marcus. "I like *them* both." _____

9. "Some days I *am* in a city mood, and some days I am in a country mood." _____

10. "*They* are both fun in their own way," said Ms. Jackson. _____

Homework

My Biggest Challenge

Write two paragraphs of five to eight simple sentences each that describe a challenge you faced. Highlight at least four subjects (S), four predicates (P), and four objects (O). Write the initial of the part of speech above the word. Give your story an original title. Make an outline in this space before you write.

_____

_____

_____

_____

_____

_____

_____

_____

_____

Scoring Rubric

1. **Top form (You're a champ!)**	2. **Fair (Keep trying!)**	3. **Needs improvement (Don't give up! You can do it!)**
Composes an original title	Composes a fairly interesting title	Composes uninteresting title
Highlights four subjects, four predicates, and four objects	Highlights at least three subjects, three predicates, and three objects	Highlights no more than two subjects, two predicates, and two objects
Writes excellent topic sentence for each paragraph	Writes good topic sentence for each paragraph	Writes fair-to-poor topic sentence for each paragraph
Supports each topic sentence with least three details	Supports each topic sentence with at least three details	Supports each topic sentence with fewer than three details
Writes paragraphs that have a beginning, middle, and end	Writes paragraphs that have a beginning, middle, and end	Writes paragraphs that do not have a distinct beginning, middle, and end
Makes no spelling errors	Makes no more than two spelling errors	Makes more than two spelling errors

Lesson 2: Kinds of Sentences

- **The four different kinds of sentences explain, question, command, and show strong feelings.**

Think About It: What Sentences Do

There are four different kinds of sentences: declarative (explaining sentences); interrogative (questioning sentences); imperative (commanding sentences); and exclamatory (sentences expressing strong feelings).

A **declarative sentence** explains what is happening. A period follows a declarative sentence.

EXAMPLES

1. The waiter dropped a chocolate cream pie on my mother's new white suit.
2. My pet canary hopped on my grandfather's head.

An **interrogative sentence** asks a question. A question mark follows an interrogative sentence.

EXAMPLES

1. Would you like to order the fried alligator or the crocodile kabobs for dinner?
2. Which vegetable do you like best, broccoli or cauliflower?

An **imperative sentence** makes a request or gives a command. It is often followed by a period. An exclamation point follows a very strong command.

EXAMPLES

1. Please stop talking. (request)
2. Stop throwing paper airplanes! (command)

An **exclamatory sentence** shows strong feeling or excitement. Follow it with an exclamation point.

EXAMPLES

1. That hungry bear is looking at us!
2. Get some towels! My bubble bath is overflowing!

Picture It

Label the types of sentences below in the space provided after each sentence. Use this code: declarative (D), interrogative (INT), imperative (IMP), exclamatory (E).

Instant S'Mores

What a hot day it was today! _____ My dad told us he had once fried an egg on a pavement when it was 100 degrees. _____My brother and I decided to do our own experiment. _____ We brought marshmallows, graham crackers, and chocolate bars outside. _____ Then we slapped everything together into sandwiches. _____ In five minutes, we had instant S'mores! _____

"Try one," my brother said, handing me the gooey delight. _____ "Can you believe that we didn't even need a microwave?" _____

Practice

Decide which type of sentence each of the following is. In the space at the end of each line, write either declarative (D), interrogative (INT), imperative (IMP), or exclamatory (E). Score 10 points for each correct answer. **Score** _____

1. I love to sleep late on weekends. _____
2. This weekend was no exception. _____
3. My younger sister had other plans for me, however. _____
4. Do you know what it's like to be in a sound sleep and to have someone slam a pot with a spoon next to your ear? _____
5. That is exactly what my little sister did! _____
6. "Stop!" I shouted, pulling the covers over my head. _____
7. "Will you read me a book?" she asked sweetly. _____
8. "Come back this afternoon," I said. _____
9. "I can't," she said sadly. "I like to take a nap in the afternoon." _____
10. "And I like to take a nap in the morning," I said, as she handed me the book. _____

 *Homework*

Report: A Lesson Learned

Interview a parent or a grandparent about an important lesson he or she learned in life. Write a two-paragraph report of five to eight sentences each based on your interview. Write the name of the person you interviewed, and tell how he or she is related to you. Use at least one of each type of sentence: declarative (D), interrogative (INT), imperative (IMP), and exclamatory (E). Write the abbreviation for the type of sentence above the sentence. Make notes for your interview in this space.

_____

_____

_____

_____

_____

_____

_____

_____

_____

_____

_____

_____

_____

_____

_____

Warm-up: Make Sense with Sentences

- **The predicate or verb is the action word in a sentence.**
- **To find the subject of a sentence, ask *who* or *what* before the predicate.**
- **Sometimes the subject of a sentence is *you*, even though it isn't written. We call this *you understood*.**
- **A simple sentence has a subject and a predicate.**
- **A simple sentence has one complete thought.**
- **Sometimes a simple sentence has an object.**
- **To find the object, ask *whom* or *what* after the predicate.**
- **Use the object pronouns *me*, *him*, *her*, *you*, *it*, *us*, and *them* as direct objects following action verbs.**
- **There are four different kinds of sentences: declarative, interrogative, imperative, and exclamatory.**
- **A declarative sentence explains.**
- **An interrogative sentence asks a question.**
- **An imperative sentence makes a request or gives a command.**
- **An exclamatory sentence expresses strong feelings or excitement.**

Relay Race

Score five points for each correct answer. **Score _____**

Part 1: Write whether the word(s) in *italics* is the subject (S), predicate (P), or object (O) of the sentence. Also, write OP for object pronoun.

1. Alicia and Pedro *wondered* when the snow would stop. _____
2. *School* had already been closed for three days. _____
3. Cars and buses *were stuck* in snowdrifts. _____
4. For a while they had fun. They built snow *forts*. _____
5. *They* had a snowball fight with friends. _____
6. They *made* snow angels. _____
7. Now *they* were getting bored. _____
8. Mom was asking *them* to shovel the driveway. _____
9. *Dad* was asking them to clean their rooms. _____
10. They hadn't even started their *homework* yet. _____
11. The cat *wanted* its litter changed. _____
12. School *was* definitely more fun than being stuck in a snowstorm. _____

Part 2: Choose the correct object pronoun for each sentence. Write it in the space provided at the end of the line.

13. My neighbor asked him and (I/me) to mow her lawn. _____

14. The movie terrified Joe and (she/her). _____

15. The coach tested Mike and (he/him) on their pitching skills. _____

Part 3: Write whether each of the sentences below is declarative (D), interrogative (INT), imperative (IMP), or exclamatory (E).

16. Did you ever go to a friend's house and not like the dinner? _____

17. One night my friend's mom served roasted pheasant. _____

18. The thought of that poor bird perched on the serving platter broke my heart! _____

19. I told my friend's mom that I was a vegetarian and couldn't eat meat. _____

20. "Eat this leftover boiled octopus then," she said. _____

Make the Connection with Conjunctions

Lesson 1: Conjunctions Connect Words and Ideas

- **Coordinating conjunctions link together words and ideas in sentences and paragraphs.**

Think About It

The coordinating conjunctions *and*, *but*, and *or* link together words and ideas in sentences. We call two or more subjects joined by a conjunction a **compound subject.** Use a plural verb with a compound subject joined by *and*.

Use a singular verb with a compound subject that is thought of as one idea (fish and chips, spaghetti and meatballs). Also, use a singular verb with compound subjects joined by *or*.

EXAMPLES

Compound Subject Joined by *and*
Shane and Danielle are the friendliest people in my class.
Conjunction: and
Compound Subject: Shane and Danielle
Use plural verb *are*.

Compound Subject (One Idea)
Cookies and milk is a delicious snack.
Conjunction: and
Compound Subject: cookies and milk

In this example, cookies and milk, the compound subject, is thought of as one idea. Use a singular verb (in this case, *is*) with a singular subject. Can you think of other examples of compound subjects like cookies and milk?

Compound Subject Joined by *or*
Luke or Corey is a good dance partner.
Conjunction: or
Compound Subject: Luke or Corey
Use singular verb *is*.

Think About It

We call two or more predicates joined with a conjunction a **compound predicate**.

> **EXAMPLES**
>
> 1. The friendly poodle ran and jumped when he saw us.
>
>   Conjunction: and
>
>   Compound Predicate: ran and jumped
>
> 2. The friendly poodle ran around the room and jumped into our laps when he saw us.
>
>   Conjunction: and
>
>   Compound Predicate: *ran* and *jumped* (In this example, *ran* and *jumped* are the predicates. Two prepositional phrases [*around the room, into our laps*] have been added to each predicate to add description to the sentence.)

Picture It

Use the spaces at the ends of the sentences below to tell whether the words in *italics* are compound subjects (CS) or compound predicates (CP). **Note:** You may see other words in between the predicates.

A Visit to Remember

Madison and *Ali*, who were cousins, took a train to New York City to visit their grandmother. _____ Gram used to *sing* and *dance* on Broadway. _____When they got there, Gram served them sandwiches and iced tea. After they ate, they saw old movies of Gram *crying*, *singing*, and *laughing* on stage. _____ Then the two *cousins* and their *grandmother* looked at her scrapbook. _____ Before the evening ended, Gram *took* out her old costumes and *modeled* them for the girls. _____ The girls *tried on* the costumes and *danced* around the room, pretending they were famous actresses like Gram. _____ When the clock struck nine, *Gram* and the *girls* took a cab to the train station. _____ Gram said that the next time they visited, they would *see* a play and *go* backstage. _____

Practice

In the space at the end of the line, write whether the *italicized* words are compound subjects (CS) or compound predicates (CP). Score 10 points for each correct answer. **Score** _____

1. *Miss Bessie* and her sister, *Miss Laura*, make the best sweet potato pie in town. _____

2. My *brother* and *I* tried it one day and asked for their secret recipe. _____

3. "You can *cry* and *beg* all you want, but we won't give away our secret," said Miss Bessie. _____

4. "We can *pay* you or *give* you one of our secret recipes in exchange," my brother said to the sisters. _____

5. *Miss Bessie* and *Miss Laura* looked at each other and smiled. _____

6. "Would you *mow* our lawn and *sweep* our porch if we give you the recipe?" Miss Laura asked. _____

7. "We will *mow* the lawn, *sweep,* and *cook* you our famous hot dog and bean supper if you tell us," I said. _____

8. "Very well, then," said Miss Bessie. "My *sister* and *I* will give you the recipe, but not until you do the work." _____

9. My *brother* and *I* spent the afternoon mowing, sweeping, and cooking. We couldn't wait for our reward. _____

10. The two sisters *marched* to the freezer and *opened* it. "Here is our secret," Miss Bessie said, handing us a pie. "We buy the pie in the supermarket, but people think it is our recipe. That is why we call it our secret recipe!" _____

 *Homework*

Thinking in a New Way

Write a two-paragraph personal narrative (five to eight sentences for each paragraph) about something that happened in your life that made you think differently. Write two simple sentences with compound subjects and two simple sentences with compound predicates.

Underline the compound subjects and predicates and circle the conjunctions. Label the compound subjects (CS) and the compound predicates (CP). Plan your story in the space below, including a title.

_____

_____

_____

_____

_____

_____

_____

_____

_____

_____

_____

_____

_____

_____

_____

_____

Lesson 2: Compound Sentences

- **An independent clause has a subject and a predicate and expresses a complete thought.**

Think About It: The Independent Clause

You've learned about simple and compound subjects and predicates. Now we're going to look at how subjects and predicates work to form three different sentence types. The basic ingredient for any sentence is the independent clause.

When you're independent, you can survive on your own. You don't have to depend on anybody but yourself. That's how it is with independent clauses. An **independent clause** is a simple sentence that can stand by itself.

Let's review a simple sentence from the previous chapter: *The sloppy student slurped his soda*. This simple sentence is a complete sentence because it makes sense. It is also an independent clause. An independent clause is a group of words that has a subject and a verb and makes sense when it stands alone.

If we took parts of this sentence and wrote them on their own (*The sloppy student* or *slurped his soda*, for example) they would not be real sentences. They would be fragments or parts of a sentence that didn't make sense. A sentence must have a subject and a predicate and it must make sense, or you can't call it a sentence.

EXAMPLES

Simple Sentence: One Subject and One Predicate

Ivan ate an entire banana cream pie for dessert.

This sentence is a simple sentence because it expresses one complete thought. It has a subject, *Ivan*, and a predicate, *ate*. The sentence is also an independent clause because it can stand alone, and it makes perfect sense.

Simple Sentence: Compound Subject

Julia and Jack rode their bikes along the trail.

This sentence is also a simple sentence because it expresses one complete thought. It is different from the previous sentence because it has a compound subject, *Julia* and *Jack*. But it is still a simple sentence because it has only one complete thought.

Simple Sentence: Compound Predicate

Tasha jumped the highest hurdle and won the race.

This sentence is also a simple sentence because it expresses one complete thought. It is different from the two previous sentences because it has one subject and a compound predicate. But it is still a simple sentence because it has only one complete thought. Like both of the sentences before it, this sentence is an independent clause because it can stand alone, and it makes perfect sense.

Think About It: The Compound Sentence

A compound sentence is another type of sentence that will add variety to your writing. We've said that a simple sentence is made up of one independent clause. Now let's create a **compound sentence,** a sentence with two or more independent clauses.

Building upon our simple sentence, we can expand it as follows: The sloppy student slurped his soda, and then he raced to his next class.

This sentence now contains two independent clauses:

The sloppy student slurped his soda
he raced to his next class

It has two separate subjects (*student, he*) and two separate predicates (*slurped, raced*). Also notice that the two independent clauses are joined by *and*, a **coordinating conjunction.** A compound sentence has a separate subject and a separate predicate on both sides of the conjunction.

The coordinating conjunctions we use most often are *and, but, for*, and *or*. Our sentence is compound, which means that we've combined two independent clauses or two simple sentences by joining them with a conjunction.

Independent Clause	Conjunction	Independent Clause
The sloppy student slurped his soda,	and	then he raced to his next class.

The main thing to remember about compound sentences is that they must have two separate subjects and two separate predicates. A sentence with compound subjects or predicates is still a simple sentence.

Ask yourself if each group of words could stand alone as two separate sentences if you took away the conjunction. If they can, the sentence is compound. If not, you're looking at a simple sentence with a compound subject or predicate.

EXAMPLES

Compound Sentences vs. Simple Sentences with Compound Subjects or Predicates:

1. Nikia won the karaoke contest, and she spent her prize money on concert tickets.

Two Independent Clauses: Nikia won the karaoke contest. She spent her prize money on concert tickets.

Coordinating Conjunction: and

Sentence Type: Compound

2. Tyrone and William peeked at the grizzly bear through their cabin window.

One Independent Clause with a Compound Subject:
Tyrone and William peeked at the grizzly bear through their cabin window.

Coordinating Conjunction Joining Compound Subject: and

Sentence Type: Simple

3. Lissett fed and watered her African violets before going on vacation.

One Independent Clause with a Compound Predicate: Lissett fed and watered her African violets before going on vacation.

Coordinating Conjunction Joining Compound Predicate: and

Sentence Type: Simple

Picture It

Label each of the following sentences as simple (S), compound (C), simple with a compound subject (SCS), or simple with a compound predicate (SCP). Use the space at the end of the line. **Hint:** Sometimes other words may come between the compound predicates.

An Old-Fashioned Night

Medora and Niesha had planned to watch a scary video. _____
They turned on the video, and suddenly the lights went out. _____
They checked the fuses in the basement but couldn't find anything
wrong. _____ Medora went to the closet, and she found a battery-
powered lantern. _____

They decided to have an "old-fashioned night." _____ Niesha's grandparents had
told them about the days before TV and videos. _____ People spent time talking to one
another then. _____ For the rest of the night, they played "Twenty Questions" and
"Charades." _____

The lights flickered, but they finally reappeared. _____

Medora and her friend decided not to watch the video. _____ An "old-fashioned
night" was much more fun. _____

Practice

Label the sentences: simple (S), compound (C), simple with a compound
subject (SCS), or simple with a compound predicate (SCP). Write your answers
in the space at the end of the line. Score 10 points for each correct answer.
Score _____

1. Gavin and his father took a trip to Cancún, Mexico. _____
2. They rode on a plane and then looked for Gavin's friend. _____
3. Diego, Gavin's pen pal, was already waiting for them at the airport. _____
4. Diego's parents gave them dinner and took them on a tour of the city. _____
5. They saw the Mayan Ruins, and they explored a pyramid. _____
6. In the evening they saw a show with Flamenco dancers. _____
7. Gavin and his friend talked about school, sports, and friends. _____
8. During the week of the vacation, the families learned about each other and became
   friends. _____
9. Gavin and his father invited Diego's family to the United States. _____
10. They would always remember their visit to Cancún. _____

 ## *Homework*

An Unforgettable Trip

Write two paragraphs of five to eight sentences each about a state or country you have visited or would like to visit. Use at least one simple sentence, two sentences with a compound subject or a compound predicate, and three compound sentences. Label the different types of sentences: simple (S), compound (C), simple sentence with a compound subject (SCS), and simple sentence with a compound predicate (SCP). Make your outline in this space.

_____

_____

_____

_____

_____

_____

_____

_____

_____

_____

_____

_____

_____

_____

_____

_____

_____

_____

Warm-up: Make the Connection with Conjunctions

- **Coordinating conjunctions (and, but, and or) link together words and ideas in a sentence.**
- **A compound subject joins two or more subjects together in a sentence.**
- **A compound predicate joins two or more predicates together in a sentence.**
- **An independent clause has a subject and a verb and makes sense by itself.**
- **An independent clause is also called a simple sentence.**
- **A compound sentence has a separate subject and a separate predicate on both sides of the conjunction.**

Relay Race

Score 10 points for each correct answer. **Score** _____

Part 1: Circle the letter of the compound sentence in each pair of sentences.

1. (a) Dylan and his friends thrived and survived in the wilderness camp.

   (b) Dylan thrived, and he survived in the wilderness camp.

2. (a) Chen huffed and puffed, and he trudged through the snowstorm.

   (b) Chen huffed and puffed through the snowstorm to his house.

3. (a) Kinesha, Beth, and Jo went to the mall, and they looked for CDs.

   (b) Kinesha, Beth, and Jo went to the mall and looked for CDs.

4. (a) Grant and his friends brought their hockey team to victory and won the state championship.

   (b) Grant and his friends brought their hockey team to victory, and they won the state championship.

5. (a) Angelia donated her old clothes to charity, and she walked five miles in the walkathon.

   (b) Angelia donated her old clothes to charity and walked five miles in the walkathon.

Part 2: Is it an independent clause (sentence) or a non-sentence (sentence fragment)? Write + in front of the independent clauses (sentences). Write – in front of the sentence fragments (non-sentences). **Remember:** An independent clause has a subject and a verb and expresses a complete thought. A fragment never does.

6. _____ Counted sheep until I fell asleep.

7. _____ Chad and his talented cousin Mallory.

8. _____ Raise your hand.

9. _____ Sharna and Ira left.

10. _____ Run!

Pump Iron with Complex Sentences

Lesson 1: Independent vs. Dependent Clauses

- **A complex sentence is made up of one independent clause and one or more dependent clauses.**

💡 *Think About It: The Complex Sentence*

Now that you understand independent clauses, the building blocks of simple and compound sentences, it's time to learn about dependent clauses. Independent and dependent clauses work together to form another sentence type, the complex sentence.

Complex sentences help highlight main ideas (independent clauses) while giving extra information (dependent clauses) to help your reader learn more about your topic. Learning this type of sentence will give your writing the polished touch of a pro.

We're going to build upon independent clauses and hook them up with dependent clauses to make complex sentences. That's all a **complex sentence** is—one independent clause and one or more dependent clauses.

✏️ **Writing Connection:** To show you how to present information in differ-ent ways to jumpstart your writing, here's an example of a compound sentence changed into a complex sentence:

Compound Sentence: Gomer made a grand entrance at the dance, and he tripped over his shoelaces.

Complex Sentence: As Gomer made a grand entrance at the dance, he tripped over his shoelaces.

Which sentence do you think highlights the sentence meaning more clearly?

💡 *Think About It: What Is a Dependent Clause?*

Now let's turn to the dependent clause. If you think of the word *dependent*, it probably reminds you of someone leaning on someone else to survive.

A **dependent clause** is a group of words that joins with an independent clause to create a complete thought. If you look closely at a dependent clause, you'll see that it has a subject and a predicate just like an independent clause has. The one important difference is that a dependent clause does not make sense by itself. You can also call a dependent clause a **sentence fragment,** a piece of a sentence, rather than a whole sentence.

EXAMPLE

Dependent Clause:

Because she was hungry

Notice that there is no period after the dependent clause because it's not a complete sentence. Your teacher would fuss about it being a sentence fragment. It wouldn't make sense unless you combined it with an independent clause to make a complete sentence.

 ## Think About It: Dependent Clause Openers

Dependent clauses begin with one of two types of words: a dependent clause opener or a relative pronoun.

The following words are often used as dependent clause openers:

after	as long as	if since	though	when
although	as though	so	till	whenever
as	because	so that	unless	where
as if	before	that	until	while

In the example, *because she was hungry*, the subject of the dependent clause is *she* and the predicate is *was*. We know that it's a clause because it has a subject and a predicate. We also know that it's a dependent clause because it can't stand alone.

Finally, it begins with the word *because*, a dependent clause opener.

Think About It: Relative Pronouns as Dependent Clause Openers

In addition to subordinating conjunctions, which signal that a dependent clause is coming up, there is also another group of words, **relative pronouns,** which introduce dependent clauses. The relative pronouns are easy to learn because there are only five: *who, whose, whom, which,* and *that.*

EXAMPLE

The mangy dog, which I rescued from the dog catcher, thanked me by running through my school.

We know that the dependent clause is *which I rescued from the dog catcher* because the rest of the sentence can stand alone and make sense by itself (The mangy dog thanked me by running through my school). If you asked *who* or *what* rescued, you'd get the answer *I. I* is the subject of the dependent clause.

Here's another sentence that uses a relative pronoun to introduce a dependent clause. See if you can name the subject of the dependent clause in this sentence:

EXAMPLE

The principal angrily led out the mangy dog that ran into the classrooms.

In this sentence, you'll notice that the dependent clause *that ran into the classrooms* comes at the end of the sentence rather than in the middle as it did in the last example.

The predicate or action word in the dependent clause of our sentence example is *ran*. What is the subject? Would you believe—*that?*

In this sentence, the relative pronoun *that* that introduces the dependent clause is also the subject of the clause. When you see a relative pronoun introducing a dependent clause, the relative pronoun may sometimes work as the clause introducer *and* subject of the dependent clause.

Let's look at another complex sentence to recap what you've learned about clauses.

EXAMPLE

The girl who sits in front of me has hair like a porcupine.

Both the dependent clause, *who sits in front of me*, and the independent clause, *The girl has hair like a porcupine*, have a subject and a predicate. The subject and the predicate of the dependent clause are *who* and *sits*, while the subject and predicate of the independent clause are *girl* and *has*. The independent clause (*The girl has hair like a porcupine*) can stand alone. The dependent clause (*who sits in front of me*) can't stand alone and is called a sentence fragment.

Even though the independent clause makes sense here, it makes more sense when we add the dependent clause. The dependent clause tells specifically *which* girl is having the bad hair day.

Writing Connection: Using Different Sentence Types in Writing

When you're not under pressure and have an essay to write at home, take a few minutes to analyze the types of sentences you write. Write the abbreviations S (simple), C (compound), and Cx (complex) for the sentence types above each sentence you write. Ask yourself how switching around some of the types of sentences you've used might make your writing more lively and interesting.

Notice how you've labeled your sentences. Have you used all simple sentences? If you have, try changing a few into compound or complex sentences. Doing this will energize your writing style.

If you've used all compound and complex sentences, think about changing the pace and stressing an important point with a simple sentence in the beginning, middle, or end of your essay.

Do you use too many of one sentence type? If so, you can add more excitement to your writing by experimenting with different types of sentences. Being mindful of your sentence patterns and working to change them can help give your writing a power boost.

Picture It

In the space at the end of each line, tell whether the words in *italics* are dependent (D) or independent (I) clauses. Highlight the subordinating conjunctions or relative pronouns introducing each dependent clause.

My Menagerie

1. *Because I've had many different pets*, I've had a lot of interesting experiences. _____

2. *Minerva, my cat, once brought me a live mouse between her teeth.* _____

3. She must have thought *that she was doing me a favor.* _____

4. *Frisky, my terrier, never liked my boyfriends.* _____

5. She often chased them around the kitchen table *until they gave up and went home.* _____

6. *Squeaky, my white mouse, used to do a tap dance on my head.* _____

7. She knew *when I had to wake up for school and would do her dance to wake me up.* _____

8. *When Slinky, my snake, followed me to school,* the teacher wasn't very happy. _____

9. *Slinky popped out of my backpack and slithered around the classroom.* _____

10. *The teacher, the principal, and the lunchroom aide couldn't convince Slinky to get back in the backpack.* _____

Practice

Label the simple sentences (S), the compound sentences (C), and the complex sentences (CX). Write your answer in the space at the end of each sentence. Score 10 points for each correct answer. **Score** _____

1. When the slimy fish jumped off the rod and into my lap, I quickly dropped it back into the water. _____

2. Buzzing mosquitoes sang to me and wouldn't let me sleep at night. _____

3. Whenever it rained, I sat in my tent listening for animal noises. _____

4. My neighbor invited me to eat a fluffy white rabbit, but I wasn't very hungry. _____

5. When night came, all the creepy, crawling creatures in the campground marched toward my tent. _____

6. I tried to scream for help, but no sounds came from my mouth. _____

7. After a gigantic scorpion crawled up my leg, I ran out of the tent. _____

8. The camp director asked me if he could do anything to help. _____

9. I told him that I wanted to go home. _____

10. Camping is fun for some people, but I'd rather stay in a comfortable hotel for my next vacation. _____

 ***Homework***

Sentence Types

Write two of each type of sentence: simple, compound, and complex. First, write two simple sentences, using them as starting points to build your compound and complex sentences.

Underline the dependent clauses in your sentences once, and underline the independent clauses twice. Circle all coordinating conjunctions. Put a box around all dependent clause openers and relative pronouns.

Simple

1. _____
_____

2. _____
_____

Compound

1. _____
_____

2. _____
_____

Complex

1. _____
_____

2. _____
_____

Lesson 2: Clauses vs. Phrases

- **A clause has a subject and a verb. A preposition has a preposition and an object.**

Think About It

You learned that one part of speech can act differently in different situations. For example, you can use a linking verb as a helping verb or a noun as an adjective. You may have noticed that a few of the dependent clause openers are the same as some prepositions you've learned (*after, before, since, until*).

It's easy to tell the difference between a dependent clause and a prepositional phrase if you remember that *a clause always has a subject and a verb.*

EXAMPLE

Complex Sentence

Before I go to the party, I'm getting my hair styled.

Dependent Clause: Before I go to the party

Dependent Clause Opener: Before

Type of Sentence: Complex (one dependent and one independent clause)

EXAMPLE

Simple Sentence with Prepositional Phrase

Before the party I'm getting my hair styled.

Preposition: Before

Prepositional Phrase: Before the party

Type of Sentence: Simple

EXAMPLE

Which is the phrase and which is the clause?

1. *After the movie* Ichabod tiptoed past his parents' bedroom because he was late.

2. *After Ichabod returned from the movie,* he tiptoed past his parents' bedroom because he was late.

Picture It

Are the words in *italics* clauses (C) or phrases (P)? Write your answers in the spaces at the end of each sentence.

Revved Up to Win

Reggie couldn't wait *until the big football game.* _____ *After school let out,* the cheerleaders and the whole school would meet in the field for a gigantic pep rally. _____ They would stay there *until the game began,* cheering on the players and creating a winning mood. _____ Reggie was proud to be one of those players. *Since grade school* he had dreamed of being the team quarterback. _____ He had practiced with the Raiders *after school* every day. _____ He was ready. *Because he had worked so hard,* his winning season was about to begin. _____

Practice

Write C to identify the clauses and P to identify the phrases in each pair of sentences. The clauses and phrases are *italicized*. Score 10 points for each correct answer. **Score _____**

1. (a) My neighbor's dog continued barking *until midnight.* _____

    (b) You may not have dessert *until you eat your pickled pig's feet.* _____

2. (a) Come home right *after the party.* _____

    (b) *After I do my homework,* I listen to music. _____

3. (a) *Before you dive in the pool,* be sure to clean it. _____

    (b) Make your special taco dip *before the party.* _____

4. (a) I haven't seen my friend *since last summer.* _____

    (b) *Since I'm interested in sports,* I go to every game. _____

5. (a) *Before my teacher gets angry,* she gets a wild look in her eye. _____

    (b) I plan to visit my brother in college *before spring.* _____

Writing Connection: Transitions can help you pull together the ideas in paragraphs or to bridge the gap between paragraphs. **Transitions** alert your reader that you're going to add a similar idea, a different idea, or a summarizing idea. These words will make your writing sound organized and logical.

Here are some commonly used transitions: *after, also, although, and, because, beyond, but, eventually, finally, first, for example, for instance, however, I believe, in conclusion, in my opinion, later, nevertheless, next, of course, on the other hand, since, so that, therefore, when.*

EXAMPLES

1. Most students take badminton or bowling. However, if you'd rather take another English course, I'd be glad to register you. (In this sentence, the transition *however* helps introduce a thought different from the one before it.)

2. Mel's mom used to make him eat vegetables. Eventually, they became his favorite food. (In this sentence, the transition word *eventually* gives a sense of time.)

3. Malik plays baseball every day so that he can improve his batting average. (In this sentence, the transition *so that* gives a sense of cause and effect.)

Homework

A One-of-a-Kind Friend

Write a two-paragraph (five to eight sentences each) description of a human or an animal friend. Use at least two simple, two compound, and two complex sentences. Write the correct code above each sentence: S (simple), C (compound), and CX (complex). Use at least three transitions to bridge the gaps between sentences in your paragraph or between paragraphs. Circle the transitions. Outline your descriptive paragraph in the space below.

_____

_____

_____

_____

_____

_____

_____

_____

_____

_____

_____

_____

_____

_____

_____

_____

_____

_____

_____

_____

_____

Warm-up: Clauses, Phrases, and Sentence Types

- **A simple sentence has one independent clause.**
- **A compound sentence has two or more independent clauses joined by a conjunction (*and, but, or*).**
- **A compound sentence must have two separate subjects and two separate predicates. Otherwise, it is a simple sentence with a compound subject or a compound predicate.**
- **A dependent clause begins with a relative pronoun or a dependent clause opener.**
- **A dependent clause cannot stand alone as a sentence.**
- **A dependent clause has a subject and a predicate. A prepositional phrase has a preposition and an object.**
- **A complex sentence is an independent clause (one that can stand alone) paired with one or more dependent clauses (ones that can't stand alone).**
- **Use complex sentences to add variety to your writing and to relate one idea to another in a sentence.**

Relay Race

Part 1: Identify the groups of words as clauses (C) or phrases (P) in the space provided. Score five points for each correct answer. **Score _____**

1. over the river _____

2. before I give my final answer _____

3. so that you will understand _____

4. since last week _____

5. after the harvest dance _____

6. that I asked for _____

7. unless I call _____

8. beyond the deepest ocean _____

9. under the basement _____

10. whenever you visit _____

Part 2: Use the code letters to tell whether the sentences are simple (S), compound (C), or complex (CX). Write your answers in the space after each sentence. Score five points for each correct answer.

11. The class was talking about careers with their guidance counselor. _____

12. Ted wants to be a surgeon so that he can save lives. _____

13. Marissa would like to be a teacher because she likes to help children learn. _____

14. Amanda finds architecture interesting. _____

15. Dinh wants to be an interpreter of other languages. _____

16. Iris wants to be an artist so that she can bring joy to others with her paintings. _____

17. "There are so many different careers that it is hard to choose," the counselor said. _____

18. "You do not have to decide now, but it is a good idea to start thinking about it." _____

19. "Every month I change my mind," said Lin. _____

20. "You have plenty of time to decide, and someday you will," said the counselor. _____

Pause at the Right Place with Commas

Lesson 1: Using Commas with Clauses and Phrases and to Make Things Clear

- **Use common sense and comma rules to help you place commas.**

Think About It

Knowing about clauses can boost your knowledge of punctuation, especially with that pesky little punctuation mark, the comma. Something else can help you with punctuation: the expression you use when you read a sentence.

If you're not sure of where to put a comma, try reading the sentence aloud, noticing where your voice pauses naturally or rises and falls. Reading a sentence aloud sometimes helps you figure out where to put the comma. But if you're not sure, knowing the rules can definitely help you. Here are some comma rules to learn. The rules are numbered to help you refer to them in the practice exercise.

RULE 1. USE A COMMA BETWEEN TWO INDEPENDENT CLAUSES JOINED BY A CONJUNCTION (AND, BUT, OR).

EXAMPLE

Yusef passed Martina a note, but the teacher grabbed it and read it to the class.

In this sentence, you see two independent clauses joined by the conjunction *but*. Use a comma before the conjunction to separate the clauses.

Note: You can skip the comma in sentences with short clauses like the ones in this compound sentence: I overate and I paid for it later.

RULE 2. USE A COMMA AFTER INTRODUCTORY DEPENDENT CLAUSES.

When you see a dependent clause in the beginning of a sentence, put a comma after it. When the dependent clause shows up at the end of a sentence, you usually don't need a comma.

EXAMPLES

1. **Dependent clause at beginning:** If Gina goes to the store, she will buy a truckload of penny candy.

2. **Dependent clause at end:** Gina will buy a truckload of penny candy if she goes to the store.

RULE 3. USE A COMMA AFTER TWO OR MORE PREPOSITIONAL PHRASES AT THE BEGINNING OF A SENTENCE.

When there's only one phrase, don't bother using a comma unless you need it to make the sentence clear.

EXAMPLE

Two Prepositional Phrases
During the first weeks of school, Mr. Wartly scowled and screamed at his math class.

EXAMPLE

One Introductory Prepositional Phrase
Before the party Esmerelda tried on six dresses. (In this sentence, there's only one prepositional phrase starting the sentence. You don't need a comma.)

Exception: In this school, teachers help students.
This sentence has only one introductory phrase, but a comma helps you avoid reading the sentence as *school teachers*. You can use a comma anytime it helps make the sentence more clear (regardless of the rules).

RULE 4. USE A COMMA WITH INTRODUCTORY EXPRESSIONS.

EXAMPLE

By the way, do you like to dance?
In this sentence, commas set off *by the way*, an introductory expression.

When you read sentences with introductory expressions, you'll know that it just sounds correct to put in a comma. Here are some other introductory expressions: *well, yes, oh, wow*.

Picture It

Tell whether the groups of words in *italics* need commas after them. Write *C* for comma and *NC* for no comma at the end of each sentence. Put commas in all the right places.

Out to Lunch

After class Hanh and Binh took a walk in the city. _____ *After they walked a few blocks* they found a beautiful sidewalk café. _____

"Would you like to stop here for a lemonade and some dessert *before we see the play?*" Hanh asked. _____

"*Yes but isn't it too expensive?*_____ My parents brought me here *before we went to the museum.* _____ *After he looked at the prices* my father said it was so expensive that we might have to wash dishes to pay the bill!" _____

Hanh smiled. "*That may be true* but if we pay our own way the way we usually do, we can afford it." _____

In the sunlight under the red awning the café looked inviting to Binh and Hanh. _____ "*Let's have that lemonade* but I feel like having the French dip sandwich instead of dessert," Hanh said. _____

Binh's eyes widened as he looked at the menu. _____ "*Wow* we'd need a bundle of money to pay for the French Dip." _____

"No problem," said Hanh. "*I'll wash the dishes* and you'll scrub the pots." _____

Practice

Insert commas where they are needed in the sentences. Write the number of the comma rule (numbers 1–4) at the end of the line. If a sentence doesn't need commas, write *no comma*. Score five points for correctly placing all the commas and five points for giving the correct comma rule. **Score** _____

1. As they sat in the lunchroom Ann and Andy began planning a costume party.

2. "It would be fun to serve weird-looking food but it would have to taste good," Andy said.

3. "Well I have some ideas," said Ann.

4. "You could roll out some pretzel dough and make twisted fingers with almonds for nails."

5. "You could shape cookies into mice and spiders," said Andy.

6. After they decided on refreshments they talked about decorations.

7. "I'll make a silhouette of you and put it on the staircase," said Ann.

8. "Since I have all the art supplies I'll make our costumes," said Andy.

9. Ann heard the bell ring for class. "After school on Monday we can get together and decide what we'll be," she said.

10. Andy said, "Oh that's easy. We'll be Raggedy Ann and Andy. We won't even have to change our names."

 *Homework*

Letter to an Advice Columnist

Write a letter to an advice columnist (two paragraphs, five to eight sentences each) about a problem you'd like to solve. Use comma rules 1–4 at least once each in your letter. Underline each sentence using the comma rules and write the number of the comma rule above the sentence. Use the space below to outline your letter.

_____

_____

_____

_____

_____

_____

_____

_____

_____

_____

_____

_____

Scoring Rubric

1. **Top form (You're a champ!)**

   Uses correct letter form

   Uses at least six strong action verbs

   Uses comma rules 1–4 at least once each

   States main ideas clearly

   Supports each main idea with at least three details

   Writes paragraphs that have a beginning, middle, and end

   Makes no spelling errors

2. **Fair (Keep trying!)**

   Uses correct letter form

   Uses at least five strong action verbs

   Uses comma rules 1–4 at least once

   States main ideas fairly clearly

   Supports each main idea with at least three details

   Writes paragraphs that have a beginning, middle, and end

   Makes no more than two spelling errors

3. **Needs improvement (Don't give up! You can do it!)**

   Uses correct letter form

   Uses fewer than five strong action verbs

   Uses comma rules 1–4 fewer than once each

   States main ideas unclearly

   Supports main ideas with fewer than three details

   Writes paragraphs that do not have a distinct beginning, middle, and end

   Makes more than two spelling errors

Lesson 2: Using Commas with Transitions, to Separate Items in a List, to Separate Adjectives, to Address People, to Write Dates and Addresses

• **Use commas to separate items, to address people, and to write dates and addresses.**

Think About It: More Comma Rules

RULE 5. USE COMMAS WITH TRANSITIONS.

Use commas to set off transitions, those expressions you use to organize your paragraphs.

> **EXAMPLE**
>
> Finally, Kira flopped down on the couch and watched her favorite game show.

Let's review the transitions you learned in Unit 8: *after, also, although, and, because, beyond, but, eventually, finally, first, for example, for instance, however, I believe, in conclusion, in my opinion, later, nevertheless, next, of course, on the other hand, since, so that, therefore,* and *when.*

Notice that many of the transitions (*although, because, but, since,* etc.) don't take commas when they're used as single word transitions. Again, ask yourself if the sentence sounds right to you with or without with a comma.

RULE 6. USE COMMAS TO SEPARATE ITEMS IN A LIST.

> **EXAMPLE**
>
> We packed the following items in our picnic basket: potato salad, pickles, fried chicken, potato chips, and bug spray.
>
> When you read this sentence, you'll naturally pause after each word in the series. If you ignored the commas and ran all the words together, it wouldn't make sense. (If you want, omit the comma before the *and,* which introduces the last item in the series.) Note: You don't need to use commas when all the words in the list are joined with *or* or *and.*

RULE 7. USE COMMAS TO SEPARATE TWO OR MORE ADJECTIVES IF YOU COULD PUT THE WORD *AND* BETWEEN THE ADJECTIVES.

EXAMPLES

1. The mosquito is a fast, sneaky, itchy bug.

2. Marv won't part with his old, dirty, magical sneakers.

3. My helpless toy poodle barely escaped from the angry, wild-eyed, monstrous attack dog.

We think of toy poodle as a single unit. That's why we don't put a comma between *helpless* and *toy*. In the second part of this sentence, we think of *attack dog* as a single unit rather than two separate words. You don't need a comma after *monstrous* because *attack dog* is thought of as one idea.

Remember: If the word *and* fits between the two adjectives, use a comma. In Example 3, it wouldn't make sense to say *monstrous and attack dog*, so you don't need a comma.

RULE 8. USE COMMAS TO ADDRESS A PERSON BY NAME.

EXAMPLES

1. Kareem, would you like to go to New York to see *West Side Story?*

2. Your story, Fred, sent chills down my spine.

3. Yes, La Toya, you have won a new bike in the contest.

RULE 9. USE COMMAS TO SEPARATE ITEMS IN DATES AND ADDRESSES.

EXAMPLES

Dates: On Saturday, November 24, 2000, my cat Whiskers gave birth to six kittens.

Addresses: My friend Paige lives at 95 Ocean Avenue, Ocean City, NJ 08226.

Note these exceptions: You don't need a comma to separate the month from the day (June 12), the month from the year (September 2002), the house number from the street name (219 Crane Street) or the zip code from the state abbreviation (PA 19136).

Picture It

Study the commas in the following sentences. Using the code, write the comma rule used in each sentence at the end of the line: to set off transitions (T), to separate items in a list (L), to separate adjectives (A), to address people (AP), to write dates and addresses (DA). If the sentence needs no comma, write NC.

A Difficult Choice

Efrain lives at 60 North Fifth Street, Philadelphia, PA 19161. _____ He came to this country from Puerto Rico in November 2000. _____ His prized possessions are his CD collection, his skateboard, his swimming trophies, and Hamsteak, his pet hamster. _____ However, his mother does not share his love for hamsters. _____

She once said, "Efrain, the hamster must go." _____

"I could never part with my hamster. She is kind, loving, friendly, and intelligent." _____

"It is either that messy, frisky, beady-eyed creature or me," his mother said. _____

Efrain looked at his mother with sad eyes. "Don't make me choose, Mama." _____

Practice

Put commas in all the places they're needed. Using the following abbreviations, write the comma rule in the space at the end of the line:

T—to separate transitions
L—to separate items in a list
A—to separate adjectives
AP—to address people
DA—to write dates and addresses
NC—no commas needed

Score five points for placing commas in the right places and five points for writing the comma rule. **Score** _____

1. Maria was looking for a low-cost round trip to Punta Cana. _____

2. There were not however any tickets available when she was on vacation. _____

3. She wrote to her sister Mirta at 96 Rose Lane San Francisco CA 60828, asking her if she could find tickets for her. _____

4. On April 5 her sister wrote back saying she found tickets on the internet at a perfect price. _____

5. "How much are they Mirta?" Maria asked. _____

6. "The tickets are reasonable and exactly what you wanted," her sister answered. _____

7. "They are I believe the best deal you will ever get." _____

8. "Mirta why won't you just tell me how much the tickets are?" Maria asked. _____

9. "I will mail them to your home at 53 Grand Avenue New Haven CT 20683," Mirta said. _____

10. "If you must know, I didn't spend a penny for the tickets," said Mirta. "I won them in a contest. I wrote an essay about why my kind intelligent and thrifty sister deserves a trip to Punta Cana." _____

Homework

Write two sentences for each comma rule. Circle all the commas.

1. Transitions _____

_____

_____

_____

2. To Separate Items in a List _____

_____

_____

_____

3. To Separate Adjectives _____

_____

_____

_____

4. To Address People _____

_____

_____

_____

5. To Write Dates _____

_____

_____

_____

6. To Write Addresses _____

_____

_____

_____

Warm-up: Pause at the Right Place with Commas

Use a comma:

1. **Between two independent clauses joined by a conjunction**
2. **After introductory dependent clauses**
3. **After two or more prepositional phrases at the beginning of a sentence**
4. **With introductory expressions**
5. **With transitions**
6. **To separate items in a list**
7. **To separate two or more adjectives in front of a noun**
8. **To address a person by name**
9. **To separate items in dates and addresses**

Relay Race

Put commas in the following sentences. Write NC if there is no comma. Write the number of the comma rule from the Warm-up for each sentence in the space after the sentence. Score five points for putting all commas in the right places and five points for giving the number of the correct comma rule. **Score** _____

1. I visited my friend Jeff at The Happy Hooligan Camp 217 Vista Street Morgantown FL 07638. _____
2. Finally we arrived at the wooded campsite. _____
3. My friend welcomed Mom and me and he invited us to a barbecue. _____
4. For dinner we ate hot dogs fruit salad corn on the cob and cherry pie. _____
5. After we finished eating we roasted marshmallows on the fire. _____
6. I hadn't seen Jeff since June 15 2000 when school let out for the year. _____
7. "Jeff I can't wait until you come home so that we can play baseball," I said. _____
8. "I will be glad to come home," Jeff said. "I've been bitten by mosquitoes flies spiders and hopping bugs." _____
9. "At least the food is good and the campfire is warm," I said. _____
10. "All I know is that home is more fun than here. I can't wait until I return to 21 Whistletown Way Sarasota FL 34235." _____

March It Out with Punctuation

Lesson 1: End Marks

- **End marks tell you the purpose of a sentence: to make a statement, to ask a question, or to show strong emotion.**

Think About It

Period: End a sentence that explains (declarative sentence) with a period.

> **EXAMPLE**
>
> My neighbor brought me back a coconut from the islands.

Question Mark: Use a question mark with an interrogative (questioning) sentence.

> **EXAMPLE**
>
> Did those red hot chili peppers burn your mouth?

Exclamation Point: Follow a commanding sentence with a period or an exclamation point. If you want to show super strong feelings, use an exclamation point.

> **EXAMPLES**
>
> 1. Please let go of that pork roast, Miss Kitty.
> 2. Let go of that pork roast, Miss Kitty!

Always follow an exclamatory sentence (sentence that expresses strong feelings) with an exclamation point.

> **EXAMPLE**
>
> "You're in my way!" the bully shouted.

Picture It

Write the correct end mark in the space at the end of each line. Where there are two spaces, write two different end marks you can use.

The Play's the Thing

1. Are you going to try out for the school play _____

2. Nothing can compare to the friendship, the stage lights, and the thrill of opening night _____ (or) _____

3. If you forget your lines, there's no need to worry _____

4. The prompter is hiding behind the curtain backstage, waiting to help _____

5. If you don't hear the prompter, you can always ad lib or make up your own lines. Sometimes what players make up is better than what is in the script _____ (or) _____

6. Before every play my friends always shout, "Break a leg _____"

7. What does that mean to me _____

8. It means do the best job I can _____

9. Best of all, acting is great fun _____ (or) _____

10. Would you like to sign up for drama _____

Practice

Write the correct end mark in the space at the end of each line. Where there are two spaces, write two different end marks you can use. Score 10 points for each correct answer. **Score** _____

1. "Kindly clean your room before you go out _____ "

2. Did your dad ever use those words to you _____

3. It's hard to refuse when you're asked in a nice way to do something _____

4. Household chores are my least favorite thing to do _____ (or) _____

5. I'd rather do twenty pages of grammar homework than clean _____ (or) _____

6. Do you know how long it takes to hang up twenty outfits _____

7. Imagine a room that is so messy you have to tiptoe through it so you don't fall on your face _____ (or) _____

8. My dog once cried until I let him out of my room _____

9. My dad sends my little brother there for time-out, and he begs for another punishment _____

10. As I tell you this story, I hear my dad holler, "Clean your room before you go out _____ " I guess I'd better start moving.

 *Homework*

A Learning Experience

Write a two-paragraph (five to eight sentences each) anecdote, or brief, entertaining story, about something that happened to you. Tell what you learned by your experience. Use each end mark (period, question mark, and exclamation point) at least once each. Circle the end mark. Write your outline in the space below.

_____

_____

_____

_____

_____

_____

_____

_____

_____

_____

_____

_____

Scoring Rubric

1. **Top form (You're a champ!)**	2. **Fair (Keep trying!)**	3. **Needs improvement (Don't give up! You can do it!)**
Uses at least six strong action verbs	Uses at least five strong action verbs	Uses four or fewer strong action verbs
Uses a period, a question mark, and an exclamation point at least once each	Uses a period, a question mark, and an exclamation point at least once each	Uses a period, a question mark, and an exclamation point fewer than once each
Writes excellent topic sentence for each paragraph	Writes good topic sentence for each paragraph	Writes fair-to-poor topic sentence for each paragraph
Supports each topic sentence with at least three details	Supports each topic sentence with at least three details	Supports each topic sentence with fewer than three details
Writes paragraphs that have a beginning, middle, and end	Writes paragraphs that have a beginning, middle, and end	Writes paragraphs that do not have a distinct beginning, middle, and end
Writes an excellent ending that summarizes what was learned	Writes a good ending that summarizes what was learned	Writes a fair-to-poor ending that does not summarize what was learned
Makes no spelling errors	Makes no more than two spelling errors	Makes more than two spelling errors

Lesson 2: Semicolon, Colon, Quotation Marks

- **Semicolons take the place of conjunctions. Colons tell us to note what follows. Quotation marks surround a person's exact words.**

 ## *Think About It: Semicolon*

Use a semicolon to join independent clauses that are closely related in thought. The semicolon takes the place of a conjunction (*and, but, or*). Ask yourself if you can separate the clauses into two separate sentences. If you can, you can use a semicolon.

EXAMPLES

1. The players met on the football field; each team was ready to win.

2. The sun shined and the ocean was warm; it was a great day for a picnic on the beach.

 ## *Think About It: Colon*

RULE 1. USE A COLON TO INTRODUCE A LIST, ESPECIALLY WHEN THE LIST COMES AFTER EXPRESSIONS LIKE *AS FOLLOWS* AND *THE FOLLOWING*.

EXAMPLE

Mr. Grizwald found the following under Wally's desk: a note his friend had passed him in class; a rotten banana and a moldy peanut butter sandwich; and a note for the teacher from his mother. (*Notice that there are semicolons rather than commas between the items in the list. Use semicolons instead of commas when the items in the list are long.*)

Note: You don't need a colon before a list that follows a verb or a preposition.

EXAMPLE

The family's hurricane shelter included food supplies, clothes, water, and flashlights. (*Included* is a preposition.)

RULE 2. USE A COLON TO INTRODUCE A LONG QUOTE OR STATEMENT.

EXAMPLE

A writer once said: "Whatever you can do or dream, you can begin it. Boldness has genius, power, and magic in it."

RULE 3. USE A COLON BETWEEN INDEPENDENT CLAUSES WHEN THE SECOND CLAUSE EXPLAINS THE FIRST CLAUSE.

EXAMPLE

Malik is a talented young man: He plays drums, bakes great desserts, and tutors children.

Think About It: Quotation Marks

Put quotation marks before and after a person's exact words. We call this a direct quotation. Begin a direct quotation with a capital letter.

EXAMPLES

1. My teacher said, "Whatever you're daydreaming about can't possibly be as interesting as punctuation."

2. Tatiana asked, "Why do some frogs take on the same color as their surroundings?"

Interrupted Quotation: When you divide a quoted sentence into two parts with an interrupting expression such as *he said, she asked*, etc., begin the second part of the sentence with a small letter.

EXAMPLES

1. "I'm proud to announce," the coach said, "that Holly scored three goals in the game."

2. "For your lifesaving certificate," the teacher explained, "you'll have to swim twenty laps and dive off the high dive."

Note: If the second part of a broken quotation begins a new sentence, use a capital letter.

EXAMPLE

"My favorite video has just started," Corey said. "You won't want to miss the beginning."

Indirect Quotation: An indirect quotation tells *about* what a person said. It is not a person's exact words. An indirect quotation does not need quotation marks.

EXAMPLES

1. My teacher said that the student who told us to drop our books on the floor at ten o'clock would have to do one hundred push-ups.

2. Rocco asked Vanessa if she would go to the wrestling match with him.

Can you make these two sentences direct quotations? You may want to drop and add some words and change verb tenses.

 ## Think About It: Punctuation Marks Inside the Quotes

Put commas and periods *inside* the quotation marks. Question marks and exclamation marks go inside the quotation marks *if they're part of the quote.* Look at the dialogue below.

Note: When you write dialogue, start a new paragraph every time the speaker changes.

EXAMPLES

1. "Hurry up! We'll miss the bus!" said Krista.

2. "I never saw you so anxious to get to school," said Felix.

3. "Don't you know what today is?" asked Krista. "We're having a surprise birthday party for Mr. Lopez."

 ## Think About It: Punctuation Marks Outside the Quotes

Put question marks and exclamation points outside the quotation marks if they're not part of the quotation. Read the dialogue below.

EXAMPLES

1. Never say, "I won't pass this course"!

2. Is that what Ms. Chan meant when she said, "Perseverance always pays"?

Picture It

At the end of each sentence, write a plus (+) if it is punctuated correctly. If it is punctuated incorrectly, write a minus (−). All punctuation marks are included.

A Class Act

Class was always exciting in Ms. Lacey's room because of the following, games, contests, rewards, plays, and pizza parties. _____ Our teacher always smiled at us as we came in the room and she gave us stickers when we did good work. _____ Ms. Lacey said that she loved our class because we were funny, polite, attentive, and respectful. _____

Last week we decided to repay Ms. Lacey for all she had done for us. I wondered what she'd say when she found out we had named her "Queen for a Day"!_____ As it happened, her face turned red and she began to cry when she saw the card and presents we'd given her. _____

"This is the best surprise I've ever had," she said, "now I have a surprise for you." _____

Did I hear her say, "No homework for a month?" _____ No such luck!

"You're all invited to my house this weekend." she said, "we'll have a picnic and swim in the pool." _____

That's even better than hearing her say, "No homework for a month"!

_____

Practice

Circle the letter of the correctly punctuated sentence in each pair of sentences. Score 10 points for each correct answer. **Score** _____

1. (a) Did the teacher say, "I'm not sure of the answer"?

   (b) Do you know why the principal said, "Stay after school?"

2. (a) I contributed the following desserts to the sleepover: cake, cookies, ice cream, and candy.

   (b) The honor roll included the following students in my class, Katia, Denise, Edward, Dupree, and Willie.

3. (a) George Washington Carver said, "Ninety-nine percent of the failures come from people who have the habit of making excuses."

   (b) It was Socrates who said: "The nearest way to glory is to strive to be what you wish to be thought to be."

4. (a) "Choose a restaurant for your birthday," my friend said, "I'll take you there.

   (b) "If you want to play video games," Dionne said, "come to my house after school.

5. (a) "I wonder what the cafeteria is serving today," said Chanel. "I like the salad bar better than the shepherd's pie."

   (b) "I run three miles every day," Jamar said. "it keeps me in shape for the track team.

6. (a) Mr. Frisby said that there are many reasons for learning about grammar, to help you speak correctly, write correctly, and to give you confidence in using the language.

   (b) The drama director summed up her message in a few words: "Make the audience cry. Inspire them. Make them laugh. As long as you move them in some way, you've succeeded."

7. (a) Always say, "I can do it!"

   (b) Did the dog catcher say, "I give up?"

8. (a) Lien asked, "Would you like to play some computer games?"

   (b) Tia exclaimed, "I'm excited about winning the basketball trophy"!

9. (a) The principal said "If you read ten books by December, I'll eat a chocolate-covered spider"!

   (b) My dad hollered, "I'm cooking a delicious breakfast of creamed chipped beef for you and your friends!"

10. (a) Did your grandmother say, "I lift ten pound weights every day?"

    (b) Did I hear you say, "If you spend all day playing video games, your brain will turn to mush"?

Homework

Write a *short* short story of two paragraphs (six to eight sentences each) on a topic of your choice. Work to create a single mood or effect. Use at least one semicolon or colon, and at least three quotations. Include at least one interrupted direct quotation and one indirect quotation. Circle all punctuation marks including quotation marks. Label direct quotations (D) and indirect quotations (I). Remember to start a new paragraph every time the speaker changes. Use the space below to outline your story. Begin by composing an interesting title for your story.

_____

_____

_____

_____

_____

_____

_____

_____

_____

_____

_____

_____

_____

_____

_____

_____

_____

Warm-up

- **End a declarative sentence with a period.**
- **Use a question mark with an interrogative sentence.**
- **Follow a command sentence with a period or an exclamation point.**
- **Follow an exclamatory sentence with an exclamation point.**
- **Use a semicolon to join independent clauses that are closely related in thought.**
- **A semicolon takes the place of a conjunction (*and, but, or*).**
- **Use a colon before a list, especially when the list comes after expressions like *as follows* and *the following*.**
- **Put quotation marks around a person's exact words.**
- **When you divide a quoted sentence into two parts, begin the second part of the sentence with a small letter.**
- **If the second part of a broken quotation begins a new sentence, use a capital letter.**
- **An indirect quotation tells *about* what a person said. It is not someone's exact words.**
- **Don't put quotation marks around an indirect quotation.**
- **Put commas or periods inside the quotation marks.**
- **Question marks and exclamation points go inside the quotation marks if they're part of the quotation.**
- **Question marks and exclamation points go outside the quotation marks if they're not part of the quotation.**

Relay Race

If the following sentences are punctuated correctly, write a plus (+) in the space after each sentence. If they are not punctuated correctly, write a minus (−). Score 10 points for each correct answer. **Score** _____

1. "Troy told his friend Selena that he wanted to see a funny movie." _____

2. "We'll go," Selena said. "If you promise not to laugh your silly hyena laugh". _____

3. "Will you promise," Troy asked, "not to blow huge bubbles and burst them in my face?" _____

4. "I'm not making any promises"! Selena said, "you were the one the usher hollered at last time." _____

5. "When you started blowing noisy bubbles with your straw, he asked you to leave." _____

6. "You said you wouldn't do it again, and he gave you another chance," Selena said. _____

7. "I was just trying to get in the spirit of the silly movie," Troy said, "that usher treated me like a criminal." _____

8. "Maybe we should go see a horror flick instead," Selena said. "What would you like to see?" _____

9. I'd prefer to see any of the following kinds of movies; adventure, romance, comedy, or drama, Troy said. _____

10. "Selena said that since they couldn't trust themselves not to laugh the silly hyena laugh or to blow noisy bubbles with a straw, maybe they should go to the arcade." _____

Sidestep Major Sentence Bloopers

Lesson 1: Sentence Fragments

- **A sentence fragment is an incomplete thought.**

Think About It

Sentence fragments and run-on sentences are major bloopers that can cause you to backslide in your race to grammar fitness. First, we'll talk about fragments.

A **sentence fragment** is a piece of a sentence that doesn't make sense by itself. It is an incomplete thought. If you're not sure if you've written a sentence or a fragment, try reading what you've written to yourself or to someone else. If the person you're reading to says "I don't get it," you've probably written a fragment. But it's not a problem. You can easily correct fragments by adding more words to make a complete sentence.

Dependent Clause Fragment: A common type of sentence fragment is called a dependent clause fragment. Here's an example: *that his pet pony ate his homework*. To fix the fragment, add an independent clause: *Felipe told his teacher* that his pet pony ate his homework.

Can you change these fragments into complete sentences?

1. As I walked out into the rain

2. so that she could study

3. After my parrot listened to my Spanish tapes

Other Types of Sentence Fragments: Any time you see a sentence that doesn't have a complete thought, it's a fragment.

EXAMPLES
No verb: Caffeine, an ingredient in cola,
To correct it, add a verb: Caffeine, an ingredient in cola, *causes* sleeplessness in some people.
No subject: collects rare crystals.
To correct it, add a subject: *My friend* collects rare crystals.

Phrase fragment: A phrase fragment is another common fragment mistake.

EXAMPLE
During her years at my school
To correct this type of fragment error, you can usually add the phrase to the beginning or end of a sentence:
During her years at my school, *the principal danced the "Twist" at all the school dances.*

There are many different types of fragments. How will you know if you've written one? The main test is asking yourself if each sentence can stand alone and make sense. If it doesn't, it's probably a fragment, a piece of a sentence.

 Writing Connection: Sometimes writers use fragments to create special effects in their writing. You can sometimes use fragments to create a mood or to offer a change of pace in your writing. However, it's best not to use fragments in your writing unless your teacher gives you permission.

Here's an example from a student's short story about being lost in the woods. The student uses fragments to create a mood.

EXAMPLE
<div align="center">**The Deep, Dark Woods**</div>
Went out walking with my brother in the woods near my home after dark. Total darkness with no relief from the moon or stars. We heard all kinds of strange noises: coyotes, owls and possibly a bear. Didn't know how this would end.

In this example, the first and third sentences give the flavor of the student's speech. The second sentence emphasizes the feeling of being lost in the woods.

 ### *Picture It*

As you read the story, highlight the sentence fragments.

Just for Fun

My entire school looked forward to the spring carnival. Rides, games of chance, cotton candy, and a talent show. As far back as I can remember. My teacher, Ms. Smiley, stood in a booth and let the class throw cream pies at her. Students paid two dollars to see her face smeared with layers of whipped cream. It was for a good cause. The school library.

One day Ms. Smiley got her revenge. When she had eaten her share of cream pies. She took a pie from under the counter and plastered one on my face. Just for fun. Now I knew what it felt like to be a walking, talking, banana cream pie. With a cherry on top.

Practice

Correct the sentence fragments below by adding words to make complete sentences. You can put the fragments at the beginning or end of the sentences. Remember to use correct punctuation. Score 10 points for each correct answer.
Score _____

1. after the heavy rain started

_____

_____

2. waving wildly from the convertible

_____

_____

3. the huge tractor trailer

_____

_____

4. in the haunted house across the street

_____

_____

5. Angela, the tallest girl in my class,

_____

_____

6. because Ravi wants to become a doctor,

_____

_____

7. in order to pass my English midterm,

_____

_____

8. after the party at my cousin's house

_____

_____

9. smiled at all of his fans

_____

_____

10. a cottage by the ocean

_____

_____

Homework

An Important Quality

Write three paragraphs of five to eight sentences each about an important quality people need to succeed in life. Check that you haven't written any sentence fragments. If you have, correct them by adding more words to make all your sentences make good sense. Make your outline in the space below.

_____

_____

_____

_____

_____

_____

_____

_____

_____

_____

_____

_____

_____

_____

_____

Scoring Rubric		
1. **Top form (You're a champ!)**	2. **Fair (Keep trying!)**	3. **Needs improvement (Don't give up! You can do it!)**
Uses at least six strong action verbs	Uses at least five strong action verbs	Uses fewer than five strong action verbs
Contains no sentence fragments	Contains no sentence fragments	Contains one or more sentence fragments
Writes excellent topic sentence for each paragraph	Writes good topic sentence for each paragraph	Writes fair-to-poor topic sentence for each paragraph
Supports each topic sentence with at least three details	Supports each topic sentence with at least three details	Supports each topic sentence with fewer than three details
Writes paragraphs that have a beginning, middle, and end	Writes paragraphs that have a beginning, middle, and end	Writes paragraphs that do not have a distinct beginning, middle, and end
Makes no spelling errors	Makes no more than two spelling errors	Makes more than two spelling errors

Lesson 2: Run-on Sentences

- **A run-on sentence runs two sentences together as if they were a single thought.**

Think About It

Run-on sentences are the opposite of fragments. A fragment doesn't say enough. A **run-on sentence** says too much. It rambles on and on until you want to scream, "Stop!" When you run two separate sentences together, you've written a run-on sentence.

There are two types of run-on sentences. One type has no punctuation between the complete thoughts. The most common type, called a comma splice, has a comma between the complete thought.

EXAMPLE

No Punctuation Between Complete Thoughts: Omar ran after his runaway dog he finally caught up with him at the dog pound.

Corrected Sentence: Omar ran after his runaway dog. He finally caught up with him at the dog pound.

EXAMPLE

Comma Splice (Comma Between the Complete Thoughts): Mr. Rugby's toupee fell off in the middle of science class, he calmly picked it up and continued talking about the frog we were dissecting.

Corrected Sentence: Mr. Rugby's toupee fell off in the middle of science class. He calmly picked it up and continued talking about the frog we were dissecting.

Ways to Correct Run-on Sentences:

1. **Write two separate sentences.**

   Run-on Sentence: Talia baked her friend a birthday cake it flopped when she did cartwheels in the kitchen.

   Corrected Sentence: Talia baked her friend a birthday cake. It flopped when she did cartwheels in the kitchen.

2. **Join the two separate sentences with a coordinating conjunction.**

   Talia baked her friend a birthday cake, *but* it flopped when she did cartwheels in the kitchen.

3. **Use a semicolon in place of the conjunction *but*** if the clauses are closely related in thought. Talia baked her friend a birthday cake; it flopped when she did cartwheels in the kitchen.

4. **Use a dependent clause opener.** You might want to change some words around and use a dependent clause opener to start your sentence: *When Talia did cartwheels in the kitchen*, her friend's birthday cake flopped. You can also use a dependent clause at the end of a sentence. *Her friend's birthday cake flopped when Talia did cartwheels in the kitchen.*

Picture It

At the end of each line, write *S* for sentence and *R* for run-on. For each run-on sentence, underline the word in the sentence that marks the beginning of the run-on.

EXAMPLE

1. Shayna won an award in the science fair for her project about the human brain. <u>S</u>

2. Marco came to this country from a small <u>village</u>, he made friends quickly and enjoys living in America. <u>R</u>

Be Proud of Your Name

1. "What's in a name?" Mr. Yamamoto, my teacher, asked. _____

2. "Plenty," Leila said. "I have a friend named Ebenezer, everybody calls him Scrooge." _____

3. "You're saying that a name can help or hurt you," Mr. Yamamoto said. _____

4. "Yes," Leila said. "I named my Rottweiler *Meatball* she's never forgiven me for it. _____

5. "Is anyone here happy to have an unusual name?" the teacher asked. _____

6. "I like my name nobody here has a name like mine," Parnell said. _____

7. "My name is Algonquin for 'chief,' it's different and it makes me stand out in a crowd," said Annawon. _____

8. "My name means 'pretty,' it makes me feel pretty and I like that," said Bonita. _____

9. "My name means 'slender.' It makes me think twice when I'm tempted to pig out on fast food," Kaylee said. _____

10. "Be proud of your name. Every name is different every name has a meaning." said Mr. Yamamoto. _____

Practice

Follow the directions to make the run-on sentences complete sentences. Write your sentences in the space below the run-on.

1. **Use a coordinating conjunction:**
   Carmen dislikes heights she wants to become a pilot.

   _____

   _____

2. **Use a semicolon:**
   Eisa sang the spiritual with great emotion, the audience gave her a standing ovation.

   _____

   _____

3. **Write two separate sentences:**
   The coach told Irina to jump over the hurdles to his surprise she walked under them.

   _____

   _____

4. **Use a dependent clause opener (add a word):**
   Matthew fell during the race, he quickly got up and started running again.

   _____

   _____

5. **Use a semicolon:**
   Dad called us in for dinner, he was making spare ribs and potato salad.

   _____

   _____

6. **Use a dependent clause opener:**
   Lamar's comedy routine was so hilarious, Ms. Williams nearly fell out of her chair laughing.

   _____

   _____

7. **Write two separate sentences:**
   Natasha took her float out into the ocean she glided back to shore on the high, smooth wave.

   _____

   _____

8. **Use a dependent clause at the end of the sentence:** Sarita made a colorful necklace for her grandmother she wanted to give her a special gift.

   _____

   _____

9. **Use a dependent clause opener:**
   Duane went treasure hunting on the beach, he found five dollars, a starfish, and a mysterious crystal.

   _____

   _____

10. **Write two separate sentences:**
    Mario race-walked to school he arrived in time for the final bell.

    _____

    _____

Homework

Persuasive Essay

Write a three-paragraph (five to eight sentences each) persuasive essay on a current news issue. Convince your reader that your position on the issue is a good one. Check to see that you haven't written any run-on sentences. Use the space below for your outline.

_____

_____

_____

_____

_____

_____

_____

_____

_____

_____

_____

_____

_____

_____

_____

Scoring Rubric		
1. Top form (You're a champ!)	**2. Fair (Keep trying!)**	**3. Needs improvement (Don't give up! You can do it!)**
Uses at least six strong action verbs	Uses at least five strong action verbs	Uses fewer than five strong action verbs
Contains no run-on sentences	Contains no run-on sentences	Contains one or more run-on sentences
Writes excellent focus statement	Writes good focus statement	Writes fair-to-poor focus statement
Supports focus statement with facts and examples	Supports focus statement with facts and examples	Does not support focus statement with facts and examples
Presents both sides of issue	Presents both sides of issue	Does not present both sides of issue
Writes paragraphs that have a beginning, middle, and end	Writes paragraphs that have a beginning, middle, and end	Writes paragraphs that do not have a distinct beginning, middle, and end
Makes no spelling errors	Makes no more than two spelling errors	Makes more than two spelling errors

Warm-up: Sentence Fragments and Run-on Sentences

- A sentence fragment is a piece of a sentence that doesn't make sense by itself.
- Correct a sentence fragment by adding words to make a complete sentence.
- A run-on sentence is two or more separate sentences that run together.
- One type of run-on sentence has no punctuation between thoughts.
- A comma splice separates complete thoughts with a comma.
- Correct a run-on sentence by writing two separate sentences; by joining the two separate sentences with a conjunction; by using a semicolon or by adding a dependent clause.

Relay Race

Label each group of words as a sentence fragment (FRAG), run-on (RO), or sentence (S). Write your answer in the space after the sentence. Score 10 points for each correct answer. **Score** _____

1. While riding along the narrow, winding bike trail on a lovely spring afternoon. _____

2. Romeo met the woman of his dreams. _____

3. Juliet smiled at him, he asked if she visited this park often. _____

4. Catching up to him and asking his name. _____

5. Juliet asked if he knew her brother Lionel. _____

6. Romeo said that he knew Lionel and had spent the whole afternoon talking to him yesterday. _____

7. Juliet asked Romeo if he'd like to come to her house for dinner Lionel would be so happy to see him. _____

8. Romeo said that might not be a good idea because they had spent time together in the school office. _____

9. Because the principal had caught them fighting over a girl. _____

10. Juliet told Romeo that she guessed it was fate, they weren't meant to be together because their families couldn't get along. _____

Leap Over Dangling and Misplaced Modifiers

Lesson 1: Dangling Modifiers

- **Dangling modifiers don't modify any word or words in a sentence.**

Think About It

Besides run-on sentences and sentence fragments, two other types of errors can slow down your race to grammar fitness. These errors have to do with **modifiers,** words or groups of words that describe other words in the sentence. Misplaced and dangling modifiers can sometimes make your writing sound comical. That's not the best tone to use if you're writing a report on a serious topic like Egyptian burial customs.

Modifiers dangle when they don't describe specific words in the sentence or when they appear to modify the wrong word in the sentence.

EXAMPLES

1. After jumping two feet in the air for a string, I gave my cat liver and tuna treats.

The first part of this sentence from the word *after* to the word *string* doesn't modify anything. Instead, it dangles or hangs in mid-air. Worse than that, it sounds as if you jumped in the air for a string.

Try changing the wording to: *After my cat jumped two feet in the air for a string, I gave her liver and tuna treats.*

Now the first part of the sentence modifies the verb *gave* because it tells *when* I gave my cat treats (after she jumped in the air for a string).

(continued)

EXAMPLES

2. After standing in the lunch line for 20 minutes, the cafeteria worker said that he was replacing French fries with boiled potatoes.

This sentence gives the impression that the cafeteria worker waited in the lunch line for 20 minutes. To make the sentence more clear, you can change it to this: *After we stood in the lunch line for 20 minutes, the cafeteria worker told us that he was replacing French fries with boiled potatoes.*

To correct a dangling modifier, you can rearrange the words or add words to make the sentence clear. In the next case, we did both.

3. Arranged on the table, I used bowls of candy as a beautiful centerpiece.

Corrected Sentence: *I arranged bowls of candy on the table as a beautiful centerpiece.*

You can also correct the sentence this way: *Arranged on the table, bowls of candy made a beautiful centerpiece.*

4. While eating milk and cookies, Mom talks to Amy about her day at school.

Corrected Sentence: *While eating milk and cookies, Amy talks to Mom about her day at school.*

You can also correct the sentence this way: *While Amy is eating milk and cookies, Mom listens to her talk about her day at school.*

📷 *Picture It*

Circle the letter of the sentence in each pair that contains the dangling modifier.

1. (a) While eating his cat food, Lyle noticed that Fluffy seemed sick.

   (b) While his cat was eating, Lyle noticed that Fluffy seemed sick.

2. (a) After talking to my friends, the baby began to scream.

   (b) After I finished talking to my friends, the baby began to scream.

3. (a) As we climbed the Spanish steps, the view of Italy amazed us.

   (b) Climbing the Spanish steps, the view of Italy amazed us.

4. (a) While we drove through New York, the Statue of Liberty came into view.

   (b) While driving through New York, the Statue of Liberty came into view.

5. (a) Taped to the refrigerator, Carmella saw a message from her sister.

   (b) Carmella saw a message from her sister taped to the refrigerator.

Practice

Correct the dangling modifiers in the following sentences by writing a corrected sentence in the space below. Score 10 points for each correct sentence you write. **Score** _____

1. While turning the corner a loud siren startled me.

   _____

   _____

2. To make a good batch of fudge, fresh ingredients must be used.

   _____

   _____

3. Looking out of the airplane, the people below seemed like dolls.

   _____

   _____

4. While sitting in the "thinking chair," the teacher told Maura to stop talking in class.

   _____

   _____

5. After failing to pass the driver's test, my mother told my brother to try again.

   _____

   _____

6. Daydreaming during social studies class, the teacher called on Rodney.

   _____

   _____

7. Tacked to the wall, Leroy saw a note from his brother.

   _____

   _____

8. Going up to give his speech, his nose began to itch.

   _____

   _____

9. Being very tired, the couch looked inviting to me.

   _____

   _____

10. Filled with home team fans, the visitors could not find a seat in the bleachers.

    _____

    _____

 *Homework*

Something I Treasure

Write a three-paragraph essay (five to eight sentences each) about your prized possession. It can be something you own or something that's important to you that money can't buy. Why does your possession mean a lot to you? Write your outline in the space below. Check that you haven't used any dangling modifiers.

_____

_____

_____

_____

_____

_____

_____

_____

_____

_____

_____

_____

_____

_____

_____

Scoring Rubric

1. **Top form (You're a champ!)**	2. **Fair (Keep trying!)**	3. **Needs improvement (Don't give up! You can do it!)**
Uses at least six strong action verbs	Uses at least five strong action verbs	Uses fewer than five strong action verbs
Contains no dangling modifiers	Contains no dangling modifiers	Contains one or more dangling modifiers
Writes excellent topic sentence for each paragraph	Writes good topic sentence for each paragraph	Writes fair-to-poor topic sentence for each paragraph
Supports each topic sentence with at least three details	Supports each topic sentence with at least three details	Supports each topic sentence with fewer than three details
Writes paragraphs that have a beginning, middle, and end	Writes paragraphs that have a beginning, middle, and end	Writes paragraphs that do not have a distinct beginning, middle, and end
Makes no spelling errors	Makes no more than two spelling errors	Makes more than two spelling errors

Lesson 2: Misplaced Modifiers

- **Misplaced modifiers need to be placed close to the word or words they describe.**

Think About It

How are misplaced modifiers different from dangling modifiers? That's easy. Dangling modifiers just dangle. They don't modify anything, or they seem to modify the wrong word. **Misplaced modifiers** are simply in the wrong place. Both dangling and misplaced modifiers can make your writing sound laughable.

EXAMPLE

Marvin was bitten by a dog delivering newspapers.

Have you ever seen a dog deliver newspapers? One way you can correct this sentence is by using a clause modifier: *As Marvin delivered newspapers, he was bitten by a dog.*

EXAMPLE

Debra's failing notice was delivered by a postal worker in a brown envelope.

Was the postal worker wearing a brown envelope? Try this sentence instead: *A postal worker delivered Debra's failing notice in a brown envelope.*

EXAMPLE

We caught flounder with the slimy worms which we cooked on the grill.

Do grilled worms tingle your taste buds? Most people would prefer the flounder. Here's an alternative to charbroiled worms: *With the slimy worms we caught flounder, which we cooked on the grill.*

EXAMPLE

I liked the photo of you and your friend in the Ferris wheel that you sent me.

Unless you're implying that you sent your friend a Ferris wheel, this sentence would sound better: *I liked the photo that you sent me of you and your friend in the Ferris wheel.*

Picture It

In each pair of sentences below, circle the letter of the sentence with the misplaced modifier.

1. (a) At seven years of age, my aunt bought me a go-cart.

   (b) When I was seven years old, my aunt bought me a go-cart.

2. (a) I saw that the soup on top of the stove was overflowing.

   (b) On top of the stove, I saw that the soup was overflowing.

3. (a) The fans cheered for the players in the stands.

   (b) The fans in the stands cheered for the players.

4. (a) The speaker in our classroom told us about strange insects.

   (b) The speaker told us about strange insects in our classroom.

5. (a) I saw a woman in an evening gown talking to a police officer.

   (b) I saw a woman talking to a police officer in an evening gown.

Practice

Rewrite the sentences with misplaced modifiers by placing the modifiers as close as possible to the words they modify. Score 10 points for each correct answer.
Score _____

1. The new car was parked in the garage which we had bought from my neighbor.

   _____

   _____

2. He left the campground in a small car where he had spent the night.

   _____

   _____

3. The letter was delivered by the mail carrier in the purple envelope.

   _____

   _____

4. The restaurant was recommended to us by a neighbor with fish, chips, and apple pie.

   _____

   _____

5. Tom Cat loved the salmon burgers fed to him by my sister under the chair.

   _____

   _____

6. There was a cherry tree in back of the garbage can which was very lovely.

   _____

   _____

7. Katrina saw a mouse on her way to the grocery store chewing on a piece of cheese.

   _____

   _____

8. I found a book of poems written by Pablo Neruda at the school book sale.

   _____

   _____

9. The fish belongs to my uncle that has gigantic fins.

   _____

   _____

10. We found a boom box in the closet that wouldn't play.

   _____

   _____

 ### *Homework*

Attitude Counts

For your final writing assignment, you'll read a quotation from a famous book, *Man's Search for Meaning*, by Viktor Frankl. Then you will write your reaction to it in a three-paragraph essay (five to eight sentences each). Write your essay on a separate sheet of paper.

After you read the passage from the book, think about it. What do the words mean to you? How has your attitude helped you succeed? How has it worked against you? How can a positive attitude help you now and in the future?

Follow the steps of the writing process: prewriting (thinking, brainstorming, using your imagination); organizing and outlining (brief word or phrase outline); writing a rough draft (getting your ideas down on paper); proofreading and revising (looking at content and style to improve it); and publishing (sharing your writing with your class and others).

As you write, keep the following elements of good writing in mind: strong active verbs; specific, rather than general, nouns, adjectives, and adverbs; a variety of simple, compound and complex sentences; and careful punctuation. Also, watch out for the big bloopers: sentence fragments, run-on sentences, and dangling and misplaced modifiers.

QUOTATION:

We who lived in concentration camps can remember the men who walked through the hut comforting others, giving away their last piece of bread. They may have been few in number, but they offer sufficient proof that everything can be taken from a man but one thing: the last of the human freedoms—to choose one's attitude in any given set of circumstances, to choose one's own way. (Viktor Frankl, *Man's Search for Meaning*)

Scoring Rubric		
1. **Top form (You're a champ!)** Uses at least six strong action verbs Uses specific rather than general nouns, adjectives, and adverbs Uses excellent punctuation Contains no sentence fragments Contains no run-on sentences Contains no dangling or misplaced modifiers Writes excellent topic sentence for each paragraph Supports each topic sentence with at least three details Writes paragraphs that have a beginning, middle, and end Makes no spelling errors	2. **Fair (Keep trying!)** Uses at least five strong action verbs Uses mostly specific rather than general nouns, adjectives, and adverbs Uses good punctuation Contains no sentence fragments Contains no run-on sentences Contains no dangling or misplaced modifiers Writes good topic sentence for each paragraph Supports each topic sentence with at least three details Writes paragraphs that have a beginning, middle, and end Makes no more than two spelling errors	3. **Needs improvement (Don't give up! You can do it!)** Uses fewer than five strong action verbs Does not use specific rather than general nouns, adjectives, and adverbs Uses poor punctuation Contains one or more sentence fragments Contains one or more run-on sentences Contains one or more dangling or misplaced modifiers Writes fair-to-poor topic sentence for each paragraph Supports each topic sentence with fewer than three details Writes paragraphs that do not have a distinct beginning, middle, and end Makes more than two spelling errors

Warm-up: Sentence Bloopers

- **A sentence fragment is a piece of a sentence that doesn't make sense by itself.**
- **To correct a sentence fragment, add words to make a complete sentence.**
- **A run-on sentence is two or more separate sentences that run together.**
- **To correct a run-on sentence, write two separate sentences; join the two separate sentences with a conjunction; use a semicolon; or add a dependent clause.**
- **Dangling modifiers don't describe anything in the sentence.**
- **To correct a dangling modifier, rearrange words or add words to make the sentence clear.**
- **Misplaced modifiers do not appear close enough to the words they describe.**
- **To correct a misplaced modifier, place the modifier as close as possible to the word or words it describes.**

Relay Race

Correct the sentence bloopers below by writing a new sentence on the lines below each incorrect sentence. Use these abbreviations to write the name of the error in the space after the sentence: FRAG (fragment), RO (run-on), DM (dangling modifier), MM (misplaced modifier). Score five points for naming the blooper and five points for each good rewrite of the blooper. **Score** _____

1. After the alligator crawled out of the lake. _____

   _____

   _____

2. The butterfly was caught by my sister that has beautiful wings. _____

   _____

   _____

3. I enjoyed seeing the picture of you and your parents in the package you sent me. _____

   _____

   _____

4. Cherise heard strange noises in the house, she reached for her phone. _____

   _____

   _____

5. On the narrow opening to the tunnel. _____

   _____

   _____

6. Stapled to his test paper, Brian saw a detention slip. _____

   _____

   _____

7. Dancing wildly in the classroom, the teacher ordered Harris to go to the principal's office. _____

   _____

   _____

8. We ate the steamed crabs with hot sauce which we caught in the bay. _____

   _____

   _____

9. Because the sun was so hot, _____

   _____

   _____

10. The zookeeper told us about the elephant he had befriended in his office. _____

   _____

   _____